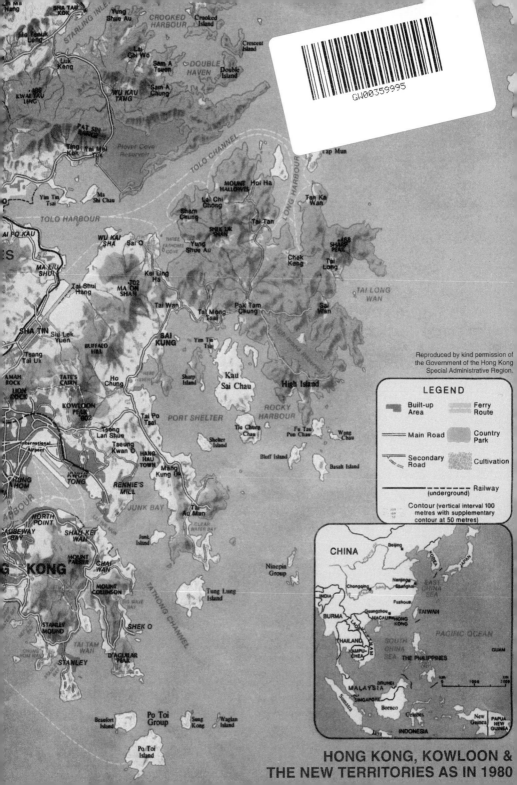

HONG KONG, KOWLOON &
THE NEW TERRITORIES AS IN 1980

HONG KONG THEN

Hong Kong Then

Brian Wilson

The Pentland Press Limited
Edinburgh · Cambridge · Durham · USA

© Brian Wilson 2000

First published in 2000 by
The Pentland Press Ltd.
1 Hutton Close
South Church
Bishop Auckland
Durham

British Library Cataloguing in Publication Data.
A catalogue record for this book is available
from the British Library.

ISBN 1 85821 773 3

Typeset by George Wishart & Associates, Whitley Bay.
Printed and bound by Bookcraft (Bath) Ltd.

Illustrations

Preface

This is an account of what life was like in Hong Kong, from a Western point of view, in the years from 1948 to 1983. It covers the post-war period when HK was to some extent still carrying on its pre-war way of life, and goes on to the formative years as the territory developed its own new identity and grew into the huge metropolis that it is today. The account does not attempt to describe the modern history of HK, nor is it intended to be a colonial servant's memoir, although inevitably there is a certain amount of personal detail as a convenient peg on which to hang description.

There may be some inconsistency in the spelling of Chinese place names, arising from my lack of sympathy with the Chinese government's '*pin yin*' form of anglicisation and their insistence on renaming places in Kwangtung in Mandarin instead of their native Cantonese. It must be daunting for non-Chinese speakers to know how to pronounce names like Zhengzou or Xiaogan when they could as easily be rendered phonetically. It is not as if '*pin yin*' evolved traditionally; it was apparently an administrative decision that could as easily be changed. There is no particular reason why place names in Kwangtung (where Cantonese is the usual dialect) should not continue to be given in Cantonese.

HK today is nothing like the HK of earlier years. When I first went there at the end of 1948, the population numbered about one million. When I left in 1983, the population had risen to about 5½ million. This increase had to be fed, housed, found jobs, policed, administered, and given cultural and recreational outlets. In the process, some of the earlier traditional way of life fell into disuse and was replaced by more modern approaches. This particularly applied to the New Territories where large-scale migration of manpower to the urban areas and to the

West led to the virtual depopulation of some villages. As a result, the cultivation of rice dropped; many rice fields became derelict and overgrown; there was increasing pressure to develop former agricultural land into profitable housing. But the process of change is nothing new. It has been going on for centuries, sometimes slowly and at other times more rapidly, usually in the face of technological progress which has precipitated a sudden change.

But change does not necessarily mean that succeeding generations take no notice of what went on before. HK is well supplied with museums patronised by adults and schoolchildren taking an interest in the territory's history and antecedents, including its traditions and customs. It is all part of the process of creating an identity and a way of life that can proudly stand on their own, both internationally and in their position in China.

Chapter 1

It was a cold and overcast day (23 December 1948), with the wind whipping up the waves in Kowloon Bay. The motorboat sailed the hundred yards to the jetty where I disembarked with my hand luggage and the other passengers, taking a last look back at the BOAC flying boat which had brought me from England. It had taken five days to fly from Southampton to Hong Kong where I was due to join the Government there as a cadet officer in His Majesty's Overseas Civil Service (in common parlance, the Colonial Service).

It had been a pleasant trip in the Short Sunderland flying boat, with a central aisle and small open cabins either side, each seating four passengers round a table. Taking off was always an exciting moment. As the aircraft gathered speed, the water rose above the level of the port holes on either side of the fuselage, so that it looked as if we were going down to the bottom of the sea. In fact, of course, it was simply the bow wave and splash coming up, not us going down. There had been a nervous time in the Mediterranean when we met an electrical storm, with lightning striking the wing that I was looking at. To avoid the worst of the storm, the pilot had brought the aircraft down to a point just above the sea, but I was past caring. The aircraft pitched and tossed, making me feel extremely unwell. I had always been a poor sailor and this was yet another sad instance of it, although the first in an aircraft. In practice, this was only the second time I had ever flown. On the previous occasion, I had been lying on a stretcher on the floor unable to see what was happening, on a smooth flight.

The approach to landing on the water in the harbours of Alexandria, Bahrain, Bombay, Calcutta, Rangoon, and Hong Kong was for the flying boat to make a few low-level passes over the water and the small vessels that obstructed the landing zone, sounding its klaxon loudly. Until the vessels got out of the way, we could not land. Compared to the present high-speed flights from Europe to the Far East, taking only eighteen tedious hours or so, the former flying boat service offered a relaxing and comfortable trip, provided you were not in a hurry. Going ashore every evening and spending the night in bed in a hotel meant arriving the other end with little or no jet lag. This was hardly surprising, bearing in mind that the plane had radial, not jet engines.

The splendid hotel in Bombay appeared to be empty of any guests except for the plane's passengers. The huge dining room was full of tables set with napery, cutlery, and glasses, as if a banquet was due. Behind each table stood a waiter resplendent in uniform and turban. It was sad that the only diners were the few passengers from the plane. This was of course a year after the partition of India and the communal riots that had driven huge numbers of the population from their traditional homes to areas amongst their co-religionists. The unrest led to the virtual disappearance of the non-Indian clientele from the leading hotels.

In the evening, the pavements in the streets around the hotel were full of prone figures wrapped in white sheets: homeless forced to sleep in the streets. Even the corridors leading to the hotel bedrooms contained rows of cocooned figures. We had to step over them to get into the bedroom.

Calcutta was much the same, but there were even more beggars. I had never seen deformed beggars before. I was horrified at some of the deformities and stopped to look, whereupon the BOAC crew dragged me away before a mob of beggars surrounded and pestered me. The captain correctly realised that I was a greenhorn needing protection.

So we arrived in Hong Kong, looking down from close range at a mass of junks and lighters sailing across the waters east of Kai Tak where we were due to land. There was the usual dummy run low over the water, with the klaxon blaring to warn vessels to get out of the way. In those days, the runway extending out to sea had not yet been constructed, so there was still plenty of water in which to taxi. For land planes, it was a different matter. Depending on the direction of the wind, it was usually necessary on landing to fly straight at the Kowloon hills, then make a right angle turn so as to align with the runway which ran parallel with the waterfront. An exciting approach for those unaccustomed to Hong Kong and possibly nerve-wracking for pilots who had not made the approach before.

The later runway extending eastwards into the sea at Kai Tak was not constructed till the late 1960s and made the approach for aircraft much easier, although it was a constant nuisance for those living underneath when aircraft passed close overhead on the western approach. All this is now a thing of the past with the completion of the new airport at Chek Lap Kok off the north-west tip of Lantau island.

Chapter 11

In the airport terminal building, there was no one to meet me. When I had collected my luggage. I went to a public telephone, found the Government section in the telephone directory, and spoke to George Rowe who was most apologetic that I had arrived without his knowledge. The airport manager was asked to convey me to Hong Kong island. This meant going back to the airport pier from which I had just disembarked and making another boat trip across the choppy waters of the harbour to Blake Pier where George and Mike Clinton met me at the top of the steps. We walked from there to Queen's Road where I was placed in a Chinese hotel on an upper floor with an injunction not to unpack, since I would be moved again next day to a larger hotel which at the moment did not have room for me. George invited me to dinner that night in his Kowloon flat, with directions how to get there. Considering that this was my first day in Hong Kong, that it was night time, and that I knew scarcely a word of Cantonese, it was surprising that I found my way across the harbour on the Star Ferry and thence to George's place. It was after midnight when I eventually reached the hotel again, stumbling up a dark narrow staircase to find my way barred by a metal door completely blocking further progress. After much banging on the door, I was admitted but passed a sleepless night since there appeared to be a dance hall directly below my room, with a tireless band.

Next morning, I followed directions up the hill to the Government Secretariat, a splendid pre-war building of two storeys with high ceilings, teak floors and ceiling fans. I met the Establishment Officer who said I was posted full-time to language study which would have to be carried out in my hotel room with the aid of a teacher. Then I was marched in to meet the Deputy Colonial Secretary, Ken Barnett, who

4

was dressed in the pre-war outfit of open-necked white shirt and shorts, long white stockings and black shoes. He greeted me in Cantonese and was visibly dismayed to find that I was unable to respond likewise, despite the fact that I had spent a term learning Cantonese at the School of Oriental & African Studies in London. (It was some time later before I discovered that one reason for my lack of progress was that the charming Chinese lady who taught us came from Shanghai, not Canton.) I was told that I would now meet the Colonial Secretary, David Macdougall, a pre-war officer who had escaped in a motorboat from Hong Kong at the surrender to the Japanese on Christmas Day 1941. He was kind and welcoming to a still bewildered newcomer.

I was then sent off to shift house to the Gloucester Hotel in Pedder Street. There I found myself sharing a large room with three other European men, some of whom changed over during the two weeks that I spent there. At one stage, my next bed neighbour was Henri Cartier Bresson, the renowned French photographer. Unfortunately, I had never heard of him before and therefore failed to take advantage of the situation. He had just returned from China which he described as in a state of turmoil with the continuing advance of Mao Tse-tung's Communist army. For several days, one of the fellow occupants was an elderly widower who stumbled back to the room three times a day quite drunk, sometimes propped up by a diminutive pageboy half his size, or by his highly embarrassed son-in-law, a Police Superintendent.

One neighbour who remained throughout the time I was there was a pre-war resident named Humphries (of Humphries Estates, a long-established real estate firm). He spoke adequate Cantonese but preferred to address the room-boy in pidgin-English which I had never heard before. Every morning, he would ask the boy to bring 'Two fly egg, sunny side up. You bring chop-chop'. Pidgin-English was apparently fairly common pre-war amongst Europeans who could not or would not learn Cantonese. The excuse sometimes given was that, if a European became fluent in a Chinese dialect, he might be regarded as no better than a coolie (i.e. a manual labourer). This, of course, was nonsense. The few Europeans who took the trouble to become fluent in spoken and written Chinese were always regarded with respect. Pre-war, cadets newly-appointed to Hong Kong were sent to Canton for two years for language study. Canton was chosen as a city where a European was unlikely to hear anything but Cantonese and where he was bound to gain a close understanding of customs and festivals. Without such knowledge, an administrator could not hope to do a useful job of work in the government. Bryan Barlow (who incidentally had been at school with me), as one of the first European cadets appointed post-war, was thus posted to Canton with his newly-married wife, but did not last long before anti-European riots in 1947 forced their return to Hong Kong and an immediate job without language training. As the next arrival, I was told to get on with learning Cantonese in Hong Kong. An elderly teacher who had over the years taught a succession of cadets in Canton was provided for me and we sat together at a table in my hotel room every day going through the exercises. A patient, scholarly man always dressed in a long Chinese gown, with traditional whiskers sprouting from a mole on his cheek, he laid the foundation of what I managed to acquire. After four hours a day of conversation and writing, I grew quite dizzy with the unfamiliar sounds.

Apart from the lack of privacy, the hotel room was comfortable and civilised, notwithstanding that the Japanese occupation had ended only three and a half years earlier. The other occupants were usually away at offices all day, except for Humphries who seemed to enjoy listening to the Cantonese training. He was most helpful in providing me with background information on Hong Kong and in introducing me to P.S. Cassidy, the head of John D. Hutchison, a leading import and export firm. It so happened that I had been at school and at Oxford with his son, Hugh, who insisted before I left England that I should get in touch with his parents on arrival. I duly did so and was invited to Mr Cassidy's house on the Peak where I explained that I proposed to get married on January 18th, the day after my fiancée, Margaret, arrived by sea from Perth, Western Australia, where she lived. Indeed, the reason why I had come out to Hong Kong by air instead of the usual month's sea voyage by P&O was to get married. Otherwise, we might have had to wait months before the next ship from Perth to Hong Kong. (HK Government Regulations in those days required a cadet to seek approval if he wished to marry in his first tour. The object of the Regulation was presumably to ensure that the cadet would not fall into debt on his initial modest salary.)

Mr and Mrs Cassidy insisted that Margaret spend her first night ashore in their house, and directed me to St John's Cathedral to meet Canon Rose, who like many of the pre-war residents had been interned in Stanley Camp during the Occupation. I arranged details of the wedding, reserved a double room in the Cecil Hotel, and went back to learning Cantonese.

In the days that followed, various people invited me to their homes, so that I gradually learnt something of their way of life and attitudes. It did not take long to realise that some ex-internees had hardly recovered from their ordeal. Conversation kept reverting to the war in Hong Kong, 'camp', privations, selfish colleagues, ill-treatment by Japanese, and a host of detail presumably to impress me. In fact, it became tedious and boring. One lady incensed me by saying, 'I suppose by coming out here you've managed to avoid doing National Service.' She was by no means put out when I replied that I had been a soldier in North-West Europe in the latter part of the War.

It was apparent that Europeans varied in their attitudes towards Chinese. The more thinking ones who seemed to understand that the War had changed values and that pre-war assumptions of superiority towards Chinese were now inappropriate were usually polite, treating them as equals. Others were not so polite; they were possibly the sort of people who would be arrogant towards any foreigner, Chinese or otherwise. But above all, it was the bustling air of business in Hong Kong that struck the newcomer. I was surprised to learn that, on release from prison camp, quite a few Europeans had deferred their rehabilitation leave and stayed in Hong Kong to put their pre-war businesses on their feet again. This particularly applied to services such as electricity generation, water supply, banking, repair of roads, docks, telephones, medical facilities, provision of housing. In many cases, pre-war records had been destroyed and it was left to the collective memory of old hands to rebuild the organisation and get matters going again. Pre-war Chinese staff came back to work, often still suffering from the effects of wartime malnutrition. By the time I arrived in Hong Kong three years after the liberation in 1945 (there was actually a two weeks' gap between the Japanese surrender and the arrival of the first British forces in the Colony), there were few obvious signs of wartime damage, such as was commonplace at that time in London. But one prominent feature of war was the exterior of the Peninsula Hotel in Kowloon. It was still covered in olive, brown and green camouflage paint.

The day came when Margaret's ship at last arrived at the P & O dock in Kowloon. But, when I tried to enter, I was stopped, not realising that I had to possess a pass issued by the P & O office on the waterfront in Hong Kong. So I took the Star ferry back to Hong Kong (about ten minutes), found the office and the pass, and returned to Kowloon. By the time I met Margaret, nearly an hour had elapsed and she was beginning to wonder whether I was running out on her. But all was well once we met. I delivered her by taxi to the Cassidys and returned to Cantonese where my teacher, on hearing my news, felt it necessary to instruct me in the different words for first and second wife, concubine and mistress.

On 18 January 1949, the day after Margaret's arrival, dressed in my best suit, I walked up to St George's Cathedral, met George Rowe who was acting as best man, and waited for my bride. Mr Cassidy brought her on time; we were duly married in the side chapel in front of about a dozen guests, consisting of government servants and their wives whom I had met in the previous three weeks. Mike Clinton lent us his flat for the reception, and I embarked on married life in the Cecil Hotel, a Chinese-owned establishment. A few days after the wedding, we returned on foot to the hotel, to find Police and fire tenders outside, with water and hoses running down the main staircase. Fortunately, the fire had by then been put out, and we were allowed in.

We had not been in the hotel a week before I was summoned to Government House to meet the Governor, Sir Alexander Grantham, a pre-war cadet who had later transferred on promotion to another colony and had now, post-war, been appointed to Hong Kong. It had been the practice pre-war for a Governor to be selected from the Colonial Administrative Service (known in Hong Kong as the Cadet

Service) and to be appointed to a Colony other than the one in which he had originally served. The purpose of this was partly to avoid problems arising from dealing on a different plane with former colleagues and partly to bring new ideas and outlook to the Colony. In Sir Alexander's case, the task of putting Hong Kong on its feet again after three years and eight months of Japanese occupation made it desirable to appoint a Governor with previous experience of the Colony, as an exception to the general practice.

Sir Alexander was affable to me in our brief interview, emphasising that every effort must be made to restore Hong Kong to its pre-war trading position and that, although the commercial side must be left to the private sector, it was the Government's business to regulate, but with a light hand. I was fascinated throughout the interview by his pipe which he fiddled with non-stop. Either side of the briar stem were metal tubes, apparently to carry off any liquid residue. As a pipe smoker myself in those days, I could understand the need for something to stop the trickle back of unpleasant liquid. But I had never seen this sort of pipe before and was somewhat repelled by its constant gurgling.

A day or two after this interview, Margaret and I were told that quarters had been allocated to us at Fanling Lodge, a pre-war bungalow in the New Territories (NT) on the edge of the Fanling Golf Course. The Lodge was intended as a weekend retreat for the Governor, but Sir Alexander did not play golf and seldom visited the place. Since it had recently been repaired and redecorated, there was apparently some misgiving in official minds at leaving a large building empty when housing was in such short supply in Hong Kong. Sending me there solved the problem, particularly as I was not required to work in an office and could therefore continue Cantonese studies with few distractions. But to make certain that we understood what was required of us, Margaret and I were invited to meet Lady Grantham, who turned out to be a small American lady, very hard of hearing, nor did she wear a hearing aid. Her particular concern was that we should not damage the orange trees that had recently been planted in the garden at the Lodge.

No time was lost in arranging for us to be driven in a government car with our luggage and stores to Fanling Lodge. This meant crossing the harbour by the vehicular ferry and travelling some thirty miles over a winding tarmac road to the north-east of the NT. In those days, there were no maps of the Colony available in bookshops, so I had only the vaguest idea of where we were. We travelled up the Kowloon peninsula, over the hills and down to the long inlet of Sha Tin. Being the end of January and winter, the rice fields in Sha Tin were bare, brown, and dry. The old Tai Po road twisted and turned with a few shaky bridges, quite unlike the wider and straighter road built in succeeding years. It was even less like the high-speed motorways that now run all over the NT. It took an hour or two to reach Fanling Lodge which lay at the end of a long drive and consisted of a large two-storey house, with splendid dining and reception rooms, and a huge garden adjoining the golf course. Uncertain and rather confused, we settled into a portion of this gubernatorial mansion, and engaged a cookboy sent to us by a Hong Kong resident whom Margaret had met on board ship. Our wonderment took a turn for the worse by evening when hordes of mosquitoes swarmed round us. The building was not fly-screened (this was done some years later). In those early days, personal insect-repellent had not been developed, so we relied on burning mosquito coils (producing an aromatic vapour that repelled mosquitoes) and on nets over the beds.

In the cool and dry winter weather, Fanling Lodge was otherwise delightful. Completely rural, the only sounds were the constant whooping calls of coucals and of black-necked starlings. We walked on the golf course, looking at the unfamiliar trees and bushes. On weekdays, there was seldom a golfer and we had the place to ourselves. A young Chinese man who spoke excellent English appeared one day and offered to teach me Cantonese, at the approved rates of my language allowance. This was a happy arrangement, giving me a chance to continue rapidly with colloquial and written Cantonese. So part of the day was taken up with language study, whilst the remainder was left to exploring our surroundings on foot. At that stage, we had no car and walked everywhere. Groceries were ordered by telephone and delivered from Kowloon. Within a few days, a European Police Inspector drove up and introduced himself. Bill Woodhead was the Inspector in charge of Sheung Shui police station which lay a mile or two away. He had been a prisoner in Hong Kong during the Japanese Occupation and was a survivor of the sinking of the *Lisbon Maru*. In the later stages of the Pacific War, the Japanese decided that, to provide free labour for industry in Japan, a number of male European prisoners should be shipped up from Hong Kong. They were sent in a freighter, the *Lisbon Maru*, with the prisoners packed in the holds. Unfortunately, the ship was torpedoed by an Allied submarine and started to sink. The Japanese crew refused to open the hatches to the holds, but the prisoners managed to open them and some escaped; many were not so lucky.

There had been some lawlessness in the NT in early post-war years, with firearms left over from the War. Former guerrillas and strong-arm men with weapons often robbed and shot without mercy. As supposedly rich people, lone Europeans were an easy target. Bill Woodhead took his duties seriously and called on us usually twice a day to make sure that we were not in trouble. Nobody in the Government in Hong Kong had told me about this, and any concern we felt was not helped early one morning by hearing what was clearly the sound of small arms fire. I recognised rifle, Bren gun, and mortar. Bill explained that it was yet another gunfight some miles away between rival smuggling gangs cutting in on each other's territory. The smuggling lay in transporting goods from Hong Kong across the border into Nationalist China which, unlike Hong Kong, charged Customs dues. The Yellow Ox gang (Wong Ngau) was the most notorious. Several times a week, Margaret and I would hear these gunfights in the distance. We understood that, despite the sound and fury, few casualties ever resulted from these fusillades which may have been intended more to scare than to kill. The Hong Kong Police of course tried to stop this activity, and in those days were armed with rifles, Bren guns and 2-inch mortars. But it was an uphill struggle that did not properly end till the Communists reached Canton in October 1949.

Walking round the golf course one day, we met an elderly European lady carrying a parrot chained to a stick. She turned out to be a German, living with her husband in a house nearby. Invited to tea there, we were surprised to be served with port and sardines emptied from a tin at the table. The Kastmann's were a pre-war couple from Hamburg. Old Karl had worked for a German shipping firm and was now semi-retired. Apparently, as German nationals, they had been interned in Hong Kong by the British at the beginning of the Second World War, released by the Japanese in the Pacific War, and then interned by the British at the end of the war. Tired of this revolving life and anxious to remain in Hong Kong, they had now taken out British citizenship. From time to time thereafter, we met Mrs Kastmann walking her parrot. She seemed quite upset when I remarked that it was she who did the walking and exercise, whilst the parrot did no more than continue to sit. I was instructed that caged birds did not need the exercise as their wings were no longer adapted to it, but they did need a change of scenery, with the sounds of nature.

Chapter III

The weeks passed in this fashion. In March, clouds rolled up, with occasional thunderstorms, and the air became more humid. We took the train from Sheung Shui station into Kowloon, looked at cars in various dealers, and bought a second-hand Ford with left-hand drive; the cheapest we could find, with easy credit terms. The car was duly delivered to us at Fanling Lodge, since neither Margaret nor I possessed a Hong Kong driving licence. She held a Western Australian licence, but although I had been trained to drive an Army motorcycle, 15-hundredweight truck, and 3-ton lorry, I had never possessed a licence for a private car, nor driven one either. In those days, the Police were the vehicle licensing authority. So Margaret called in at the Police Traffic Office in Nathan Road, Kowloon, and a European Inspector named Ross sat in our car whilst she drove it up and down the road. This was good enough for a Hong Kong licence to be issued on the strength of the Western Australian one. So she set off from Kowloon on the long drive back to Fanling. Not 100 yards down the road, a Chinese pedestrian carrying a sack of rice on his shoulder stepped off the pavement into the path of the car. Margaret braked sharply. The car was hardly moving when it hit the pedestrian who fell over, scattering the rice. Unhurt, he leapt up and took to his heels as fast as he could, presumably fearing retribution for not looking where he was going. It was a distraught Margaret who returned to the Inspector to tell him what had happened. As soon as he saw her, he feared the worst but was reassured by her story. It was not her fault; the victim appeared unhurt; he was unlikely to complain; and no action need be taken. An even more cautious driver returned home, in need of moral support.

In due course, I obtained my licence, fortunately without incident. Becoming mobile meant that we were able to travel further afield in the

NT and to get to know something of the countryside which in those days was largely rural and geared to the production of rice. Almost all valleys with constant or even seasonal streams were full of rice fields, separated by earth bunds (mounds) which often acted also as pathways. Villages were usually on slightly higher ground, provided the well supplied enough water. Village houses were built in terraces, with local thin bricks and earthenware tiles on the roof. A plasterwork curve was often placed at the four lower ends of the roof, to stop the devil from sliding down. Beams and rafters were of pinewood. To deter termites from attacking the wood, a glazed earthenware cock might be placed at either end of the ridge-pole, to warn termites that they would be eaten up if they approached. The area in front of the row of houses was usually paved with stone or latterly cement, to be used as a drying ground for rice after the harvest; for drying cow dung as a fertiliser; and for drying laundry on bamboo poles. To one side of the houses would be heaps of fuel for cooking, consisting of dried grass and bushes cut from the hillsides. Each family had its designated area of hillside, and it was one of the women's jobs to clamber up with a carrying pole and chopper to shave the hillside, afterwards carrying down at either end of the pole a large bundle of vegetation, tied together with creeper. It could be disconcerting to round a corner on a hillside path and meet a huge bundle of vegetation advancing towards one, apparently under its own steam. It was also apparent that the carrier could not see ahead and was simply watching her feet on a well-known path. If you did not get out of the way, you were liable to be run over.

Branches from pine trees were an additional source of fuel. Hillsides above villages were usually clad in grass, bushes, and small trees, with areas of scattered pine trees (*Pinus massoniana*). Traditionally certain hillsides and the pine trees on them were the preserve of particular families which would trim off lower branches or fell trees. Many families secured their title to the hillside (which remained Crown land) by the issue of Forestry Permits from the local District Office.

In the early post-war years, the rural economy of the NT depended largely on the production of rice, following an age-old pattern. In its turn, the production of rice depended on the supply of water, bearing in mind that Hong Kong weather consisted of a wet and humid summer and a dry winter. Good rice fields with plenty of water were able to sustain two crops with big ears of rice; more marginal fields only one crop. It was an NT saying that *Shui wai choi* (water makes riches). The supply of water to the fields came from hillside streams, being led off at the right level in channels flowing gently downhill. The flow of water to different fields was controlled and distributed by small temporary earth dams and wooden boards in the channels. It was an elaborate system that worked. Villagers understood their traditional areas and the sources of water. Where communities had been settled in their villages for ages, there were seldom disputes over land or water rights, because everyone knew what belonged to whom.

In the dry winter months, after the second harvest in October, the rice fields lay bare and brown. Apart from some vegetables and perhaps fruit trees grown close to the village, nothing much else was grown in winter. But, in March when occasional thunderstorms occurred, the fields would be ploughed, with an ox or buffalo pulling the wooden plough (sheathed in metal). Seed rice would be soaked in water in a bamboo basket, and then planted in a small wet patch to produce a dense mass of seedlings. When more rain came in April and May to flood the fields, the sandy soil would be harrowed to a creamy consistency before the seedlings were planted out in rows, with the base of the plant in mud under water and the top of the plant sticking out above. It was essential to have an inch or two of water in the fields throughout the growing time.

At planting time, every villager (male and female) seemed to be out in the fields, with trousers rolled well up their thighs, dragging baskets of seedlings or bent over planting in water up to their elbows, or shouting orders and encouragement. It was all hands on deck in back-breaking labour. In the weeks that followed, it might be necessary from time to time for a villager to paddle up and down the rows of rice, using his bare feet to press the mud down firmly round the base of each plant where rain had loosened the soil. It was this paddling and pressing down action that formed the basis of the traditional rice dance, which was performed with a lot of foot movement.

In July, the first crop of rice was ready for harvesting, and the fields would be drained of water in preparation. Again, villagers would be out in strength, some cutting the rice with sickles, others carrying the cut rice to the person at the thresher. This consisted of a drum-like basket with a bamboo screen round three-quarters of the top. The rice heads were banged against slats across the top of the basket, so that the grains of rice fell down and the screen prevented scattering. Finally, the rice was taken to a paved area and spread out to dry. Sometimes one side of a tarmac road might be taken over for the purpose. Since there were fewer roads in the NT in those days and even fewer vehicles, it caused no great problem. When the rice was judged to be dry enough, it was put through a wooden winnowing machine to remove the husks. Part of the final husked rice might be kept for home consumption and the balance carried to market in panniers at either end of a carrying pole. In well-watered and favourable fields, a second crop would be planted directly after the first harvest in July and in its turn would be harvested in October.

Rice was so important a part of local diet and of agriculture that there were separate Cantonese words for rice growing in the field; unwinnowed rice; winnowed rice; and cooked rice. Rent for leased paddi fields was paid in rice, measured in standard trays. Traditionally rice merchants were regarded as among the richest of merchants, combining the business for some reason with the sale of firewood. Rice shops were easily recognised by their tubs of rice standing at the entrance, each labelled according to quality and price. The experts claimed that the poorer strains of rice contained up to 5 per cent sand that clung on from the fields. The implements such as ploughs, baskets, tubs, choppers, carrying poles, etc. needed for this agricultural way of life were mostly made locally, using local material. Carrying poles for instance tended to be made of guava wood which was strong and springy. The pole would be flat so as to lie comfortably on the shoulder, allowing the carrier on level ground to proceed at a fast pace somewhere between a walk and a run. Because he could not stop in a hurry, he was forever shouting a warning to pedestrians ahead to mind the way. Since this was before the days of lorry transport all over the

The District Officer (me) inspecting the rice harvest,
with a young Hakka girl (1950).

Traditional ploughing with an ox (1950). Village houses in the background.

NT, carrying poles and human transport were the standard method of moving things about.

Villages tended to be inhabited by members of one or more clans, i.e. related people with the same surname. The vast majority of NT people in those early post-war days were Cantonese, but round the coast and elsewhere would be Hakka, speaking their own dialect and traditionally believed to have come centuries before from further up the coast. They may have been part of the forced migration in earlier days when, tiring of continual piracy, the Chinese government of the day required coastal villages further north to be cleared of inhabitants and demolished. There was little outward difference between Cantonese and Hakka. But Hakka women usually wore a black square cloth on their heads, with a red band round it for unmarried and a white band for married. Hakka were followers of animism, believing that certain rocks and trees contained spirits that needed to be venerated by means of an altar, candles and offerings. In those days, both Cantonese and Hakka men and women wore traditional black cotton jackets and trousers, with rubber thongs for shoes. Working in the fields, women usually wore a large broad-brimmed straw hat that had a black cloth hanging from the brim and a hole in the centre where the wearer's head projected through. Fishermen wore a straw hat with a narrower curved brim that was less likely to catch in the rigging. Traditionally clothing did not carry bone or plastic buttons, but instead had a knob of thick thread on one side of the garment and on the other side a loop of thread through which the knob was passed. It worked very well. The opening for women's dresses and jackets was placed on the right, not in the centre.

In wet weather, both sexes would put on a cape consisting of the broad overlapping leaves of the Chinese fan palm (*Livistona chinensis*). It was surprising how effective it was in keeping the wearer dry. (The same leaves were used for the roof of matsheds.) The feet and legs would be left bare. In later years, the leafy cape was abandoned in favour of a plastic mackintosh or even a plastic fertiliser sack with armholes cut in it.

In both the urban areas and the NT, Chinese took pains in wet weather to cover their heads, sometimes at the expense of the rest of their bodies. Caught out by an unexpected shower, it was commonplace to see people rushing for cover holding newspapers, plastic bags, or even a bus ticket over their heads. Theories to explain this practice were fanciful. For instance, pigtails worn in the days of the Ching dynasty were often dyed to keep them glossy and black, meaning that wearers avoided rain that might cause the dye to run. It was thought that the habit persisted, even when pigtails ceased to be worn after the end of the dynasty in 1911. A more ribald theory claimed that men feared their virility might be affected if their heads got wet. The more likely explanation is a concern that a wet head would lead to a cold and bad health.

Chapter IV

Not long after our move to Fanling Lodge, we were joined by Donald Luddington and his wife Garry. A fellow cadet, he had been on the Colonial course with me at Oxford and London, but had come out to Hong Kong by sea. We shared the house and tried to find our feet in the new surroundings. Our stay was shortly interrupted when, in May 1949, I was told to report to the District Office, Tai Po. There I met John Barrow the District Commissioner, NT, a pre-war officer who spoke fluent Cantonese and Hakka. It appeared that Ian Gordon-Williams, the current District Officer, Tai Po, had been diagnosed as suffering from a brain tumour. To fill the vacancy, I was to be posted forthwith as DO, Tai Po (Administrative), and Donald Luddington as DO (Legal). This split took account of our lack of training and experience. In those days, the DO also sat three days a week as Police Court Magistrate in respect of cases arising in his District. In addition, he was an Assistant Land Officer dealing with land disputes which could be heard informally; provided they were registered as a memorial, decisions were legally binding. Finally, the DO also sat in a Small Debts Court where he decided on claims for repayment of money up to a stipulated amount.

So I turned up at the District Office, Tai Po, which was a long brick-built structure with high ceilings and an overhead fan. The District Office was at one end, the Police Court in the centre, and the office of the District Superintendent of Police, NT, at the other end. Perched at the top of a hill overlooking Tide Cove, an inlet of the sea, the site of the building had been the scene of an action in 1898 at the time of China's lease of the NT to Britain. The local mandarin had opposed the lease, chased away surveyors and burnt their matsheds. His troops lined the top of the hill. Lieutenant Keyes, RN (later Admiral of the Fleet Lord

Keyes), and a party of bluejackets were landed at the foot of the hill whence they put the mandarin's troops to flight. I was now about to take advantage of his action.

The District Office, Tai Po, must have been built shortly after the turn of the century, when surveyors and staff of the District Administration had gone over the whole of the newly-leased NT registering claims to ownership of property. The results were recorded in registers and on cadastral survey maps for the District Office (North) and the District Office (South). These paper maps with linen backing showed all private land in demarcated districts, with Crown land a perfect and absolute blank. The maps that we used in Tai Po (the two pre-war Districts had post-war been stretched to three; Tai Po in the north and east; Yuen Long in the west, and south taking the rest, i.e. Saikung and islands) appeared to be the original maps of fifty years ago. The folds were creased, with boundaries inexact where there were stains or paper had come adrift. But they were better than nothing; it was a wonder that the land memorials and the plans had survived the Japanese Occupation intact. But the main point was the recording of ownership of land and public acceptance of its accuracy and value. It is commonplace nowadays to use the term 'colonialism' in a pejorative sense, implying the imposition by a Western power of an authoritative government over a native people who are squeezed of whatever can be gained from their territory.

This is a sad misunderstanding of the facts as far as Hong Kong is concerned. One of the great benefits that Britain brought to its colonies (certainly to Hong Kong) was the registration of ownership of private land. Where land could change hands for large sums of money, it really mattered to be able to establish ownership, exact boundaries, covenants, easements, etc. But, in the District Office, Tai Po, in 1949, we were still struggling to tidy things up after the War. A continual problem was the failure of families and clans to register succession where the last owner had died during the Japanese Occupation. Every owner was issued with a 'jarp jiu' (certificate of title). Some of those surrendered on registering succession and the issue of new certificates bore the signatures of earlier District Officers, including Cecil Clementi (later Governor of the Straits Settlements) and even Tratman, the original District Officer. I used to collect the old ones as historic records; I handed them over years later to the Government Archivist.

Because there was no handover from my sick predecessor, I entered upon my administrative duties as a District Officer without the faintest idea of what to do. My life till then had not taught me the difference between a minute in a file and a memorandum. I sat at the desk, looked at a piled-up In tray and an empty Out tray, and read through the first bit of paper. As it was grammatically correct, I signed it without understanding what it was about, likewise a number of other documents. In the days that followed, I gradually built up knowledge about the duties of a DO, relations with inhabitants of the District, general procedures, and traditional Chinese customs. It was George Roylance, the Land Bailiff (he lived with his mother in a flat above the office) who steered me through the maze of official papers and taught me what to do, avoiding the pitfalls. I owe him a deep debt of gratitude for his honest and tactful directions. Together we visited the District by car and examined sites which were the subject of land applications, and I was instructed in the several subterfuges to guard against.

Most of the work related to land: applications to purchase Crown land for building or agriculture, or to convert agricultural land to building status, or annual permits to occupy Crown land for some purpose, or permits for temporary structures, or permits for forestry lots on Crown land. Because the NT had been leased to Britain by China for ninety-nine years from 1 July 1898, all private land there was held on lease expiring on 30 June 1997, less the last three days. There was no freehold land in the NT.

Every NT village was in the care of a designated Village Representative (usually a respected clan elder) whose business it was to speak to the DO on village matters. These could include disputes, *fung shui* problems, and statutory declarations on behalf of villagers seeking post-registration of births that had occurred during the Japanese Occupation. A common source of dispute was where a villager complained that another was digging in or otherwise damaging an area regarded as sacred to *fung shui* (literally meaning wind and water). *Fung shui* is a belief that beneficial influences lay in certain places and could be divined by those skilled in recognising the signs. For instance, hills of a certain shape with a view of the sea could be excellent sites for graves. As a result, various hills in the NT were dotted with horseshoe-shaped graves of ancestors, in particular hills where it appeared that the spirit of a green dragon was on the left and a white tiger on the right.

Although the tiger played a large part in Chinese mythology, it could also cause problems. All village houses traditionally faced the same way, to avoid windows and doors (likened to a tiger's open jaws) confronting each other. This required careful siting of villages so as not to face each other visually, even if a mile or two apart. Proper separation had been arranged when the villages were originally founded, perhaps a century or two before. But, in more modern times, a new isolated house might fail to observe tradition, with the result that disputes arose. Villagers' fears stemmed not so much from the break with tradition as from a possible threat to harvests, illness and general livelihood. This sort of dispute was not something to brush aside as of trifling importance. Villagers' traditional belief in *fung shui* was so deep-seated in those days as to lead to disorder and bloodshed. Solutions had to be found before hotheads resorted to violence. Where discussions led nowhere, the DO might be approached, as an official with wide legal powers. Indeed, the traditional respect for a DO in the NT lay largely in his capacity as a Police Court Magistrate and Assistant Land Officer with legal powers to enforce judgments. The DO was in effect the successor to a Chinese magistrate, bearing in mind that fifty years earlier the NT had been Chinese territory. Some villages still retained the stone mountings for displaying ceremonial banners to announce a villager's success in the Imperial examinations to become a mandarin or magistrate.

The standard solution to disputes about houses facing each other was to plant a stand of bamboos in between as a screen. In the intervening years before the bamboos grew big enough, a temporary wall or fence in front was necessary, at the newcomer's expense. As he caused the trouble, it was reasonable that he should bear the cost. Matters did not always work out so easily.

As one of the two DOs, I was allocated the departmental quarters at the Lookout in Tai Po Kau, a pre-war bungalow a few miles from the District Office on a hill overlooking Tide Cove and the Pat Sin range of hills on the other side. It was quiet and peaceful, with a magnificent view. At night, Tide Cove would be dotted with the bright lights of fishing boats and the sound of oars banging on the gunwale. The lights were to attract fish; the banging to drive them into the centre of an encircling net. Two boats gradually dragged the two ends of the net together and then used a scoop to lift out the boiling mass of struggling fish. An occasional explosion indicated where a fisherman had illegally dropped a charge overboard as a quicker method of fishing. In some fishing villages, an unfortunate could sometimes be seen minus an arm, where the charge had gone off prematurely. Because fishing boats in those days used either sails or oars, Tide Cove did not echo with the raucous sound of engines and outboard motors.

On the other side of Tide Cove, in one particular bay, small octopus were gathered by lowering a line to which were attached a dozen or more cheap china tea cups. The top of the line was tied to a floating buoy. The octopus liked to occupy the cups which were periodically hauled to the surface and emptied of their catch. In the same sheltered area, abalone was gathered by a fisherman in a sampan wielding two long thin bamboo poles. One pole ended in a brass claw, the other pole in a flat wooden pad. Standing in the open boat, the fisherman felt around the sea bed with the clawed pole until he sensed a shellfish. Then, with his leg wrapped around one pole and his arms on the other, he detached the shell from the bottom and adroitly brought it up without dropping the catch. These two methods of fishing have long since disappeared from Tide Cove, in the advance of reclamation and pollution. There appears to be a factory now in that particular bay where there used to be sea. In 1950, at the side of the dirt track behind the bay, I saw for the first time a flock of lesser black-tailed hawfinches, winter visitors from China. There is a housing estate on the site now.

In those days, although some fishermen lived ashore in remote villages where they carried on some agriculture too, the majority lived on board their vessels. In various sheltered parts of Tide Cove, there were clusters of sampans and of larger fishing vessels, with whole

A view of a typical fishing village in the New Territories in 1949,
before roads and development arrived.

families cooking, washing and sleeping on board. Small children might have a rope tied round their waist to prevent their falling overboard. The Cantonese fishing community, called Tanka (phonetically pronounced Darngar), were separate from land-based Cantonese, and separate again from the Hoklo fishing community who used a different style of fishing boat and spoke a form of Chiu Chow dialect from the Swatow district further up the coast of China.

This was the era before nylon became commonplace. Sails for these fishing vessels were therefore made of canvas. Ropes were twined from fibre, by means of two fishermen squatting some distance apart on the waterfront, each behind a spindle, with long strands of fibre between them, gradually being twisted to form rope. On certain beaches, at low tide, might be a fishing boat high and dry, propped up with poles on each side. Stacked to one side would be a heap of brushwood that was fed into a fire beneath the vessel's hull to burn off the weed and shells that had accumulated there. At certain inlets round the coast were small rudimentary kilns where shells were burnt to produce lime for the

The bay at Tai Mei Tuk (New Territories) with the District Office launch in the background. This was 1951, long before a road was built there.

building trade. Access to and from these kilns was provided by boatmen who also served to carry goods to outlying areas and islands.

To visit the more distant parts of the district where there were no roads in those days, there was an open-topped launch with a crew and an inboard diesel engine, moored alongside the government pier at Tai Po Kau. It took several hours to reach the island of Peng Chau at the far end of Mirs Bay which was legally part of Hong Kong waters up to high water mark on the shore of the Bay. I thoroughly enjoyed trips to what were then remote places, to meet villagers and fishermen who otherwise seldom encountered officialdom. The Tai Po Kau pier was also the terminus in 1949 for the daily ferry from there to Sha Yu Chung (literally shark inlet) across Mirs Bay in China. The ferry service was discontinued after the Communists reached Canton in October 1949.

A Village Representative from a distant Hakka community appeared in the office one day requesting that I arrange the issue of a fresh passport for one of his villagers who wished to migrate to Britain to join a relative running a Chinese restaurant. The villager turned out to be a grinning negro with flashing white teeth and curly hair, speaking only Hakka and not a word of Cantonese or English. His out-of-date passport lacked covers that had rotted off when hidden during the Japanese Occupation and described him grandly as named something like 'Alexander Clutterbuck Featherstonehaugh'. The explanation for this unusual background lay in the fact that it had apparently been pre-war practice for surplus manpower in Hakka fishing villages to engage as crew with various shipping lines. Some of these Chinese crew then left the ship in the West Indies, cohabited with local coloured girls, and eventually returned to their native village in the NT, bringing with them any male children; girls were left behind with the mother. The boys were brought back because only males may perform ancestor worship. I was delighted to help such a splendid applicant, although it seemed unlikely that he had any idea of work in a restaurant.

Chapter V

In March and April 1949 the first thunderstorms arrived, with lightning and thunder reverberating backwards and forwards between Grassy Hill south of Tai Po Kau and the Pat Sin Range on the other side of Tide Cove. Our electricity which came on pylons from Kowloon past Grassy Hill was often interrupted by the storms. Once a lightning strike on the wires travelled down into our kitchen, with a loud explosion in the electric oven. It frightened the cookboy so much he refused to enter the kitchen again till the storm blew over. Directly after the rain from the storms, villagers at once started to plough their rice fields and prepare the seed beds. When the more steady rain appeared in May, they harrowed the fields to a creamy texture and began planting out seedlings. This rural life was governed by the seasons, with set tasks arising in their due course. The temperature grew hotter and the humidity increased. We changed from winter to summer clothes, and sought the shade and coolness. These were the days before air-conditioning. Offices had high ceilings and were sited to take advantage of through-breezes. In summer, with the windows open and the ceiling fan turning, the District Office in Tai Po caught the distant sound of human life and the closer liquid calls of black-naped orioles in the surrounding pine trees. The office also caught the sound of the new diesel locomotives in the Kowloon Canton Railway track that lay a hundred yards away. The sound was so loud that conversation, especially on the telephone, had to cease until the train had passed.

For a time, to bridge a gap, Margaret worked in the office as my secretary until Gloria Barretto took over and became almost a fixture there. She was a tower of strength in reminding me of correct procedure and in curbing excessive enthusiasm. On one occasion, I was required to accompany John Barrow, the District Commissioner, to meet the

Colonial Secretary (John Nicoll, transferred from British North Borneo) on his tour of the NT. Shortly after that, I was surprised in the office to receive a telephone call from the Government Secretariat in HK to say that the CS wished to speak to me. He came on the line to invite me and my wife to go to the Happy Valley races on the coming Saturday. Those were the days when the Administrative Service in HK numbered fewer than twenty officers, and it was possible for a CS to get to know them all (helpful if he had to countersign their annual confidential reports). So I checked with Austin Coates, a colleague in the Secretariat, that it was a genuine call and not a hoax. Margaret and I then duly turned up at the races, where we were introduced rather perfunctorily to the other people who shared the CS's box. The only other person I could identify was a Mr X, a Commonwealth Trade Commissioner. In the course of the afternoon, a lady present accompanying Mr X addressed him as 'darling', and commented on the various things they had done together. When Margaret and I eventually departed at the end of the races, I thanked the CS and thanked Mr and Mrs X, whereupon she said 'But I'm not Mrs X.' This caused Mr X to look uncomfortable, the CS looked up at the sky, and we were not invited again. Apparently Margaret and I were the only people who did not understand the arrangements. I later met the lady's husband, and realised why she was looking elsewhere. It takes a mistake like this to make one wary of using names unless quite certain of identity. It also emphasises the importance of proper introductions.

One day, a group of villagers called at the office to apply for a grant of cement, sand and aggregate from the local Public Works vote for the construction of a small dam on a stream close to the Chinese border, so as to allow water to be led off in a channel to irrigate nearby paddy fields that suffered from an inadequate supply. George Roylance and I duly visited the site which was difficult to pinpoint on the worn and tired cadastral map produced early in the century. But the request seemed genuine and was approved. George checked the work at various stages (an essential step to ensure the material was actually used and not resold) and pronounced the job completed. It was some time later that we discovered the stream in question had changed course since the

Formal photograph at the official opening of new cooked food stalls in Tai Po (winter 1949).

map was produced and the dam had actually been built in Chinese territory. We kept quiet, of course, and there were never any repercussions. According to John Barrow, a pre-war lead mine at Lin Ma Hang in the north-east NT sank a shaft northwards across the border and mined ore for years from beneath Chinese soil, without anyone questioning sovereign rights.

Villagers in those days travelled backwards and forwards across the border, which was defined only by boundary stones at intervals from Sha Tau Kok in the north-east to the Lo Wu railway bridge in the west. Some villagers who lived in China owned fields in the NT, and came over daily to work them. On the HK side of the border lay the border road, a narrow track running from Sha Tau Kok to a point near Sheung Shui in the middle. I used to drive over the border road from time to time to check on land matters. Running northwards from Sheung Shui was the main road to Man Kam To and the bridge over the Shum Chun river which marked the border in that area. This was the road that led eventually to Canton, although few vehicles in fact went that far because of problems in crossing intervening rivers. Passengers and goods normally travelled between HK and Canton by ship up the Pearl River.

Another applicant for assistance from the LPW vote was the young leader of the Hoklo fishermen in Tai Po who wanted a sheltered lagoon beside the road deepened and enlarged so as to act as a typhoon shelter for fishing vessels. Again, this was approved. It was followed by an invitation for Margaret and I to go on a fishing vessel for a short trip in Tolo Harbour. Sitting on the deck on seagrass mats, we watched as a couple of fishermen hoisted reddish-brown canvas sails and sent the vessel rushing before a stiff breeze. At this stage, I had been in HK for less than six months. Living in the NT and meeting few other Westerners, I lacked much local knowledge. For instance, I might have realised that in May/June rain is seldom far away and that it is prudent to be prepared for it. But, as landlubbers knowing nothing about sailing, we were enjoying the unfamiliar sea trip and failed to notice a squall coming across the water. The fishermen saw it, dropped the sails, and clung on tightly as we were lashed with rain and soaked by huge waves. I was sure the vessel would overturn but was reassured by the fishermen who regarded it all as great fun.

Chapter VI

As the summer advanced, the heat and humidity built up. Although the temperature in HK seldom rises above 35°C, it can be coupled with high humidity that saps energy and makes life a drag. It takes time to become acclimatised. The pre-war response in summer was to slow up, avoid violent exercise, seek the shade, and live where there was a through-breeze. Western men tended to dress in an open-necked white shirt and shorts, with long white stockings and black shoes. Women wore sleeveless summer frocks. This approach prevailed post-war up till the 1950s when air-conditioners came on the market and a boom started in real estate. Developers of multi-storey office buildings sought lower ceiling heights under the building regulations, on condition that they installed central air-conditioning. The same applied to blocks of domestic flats, except that tenants or owners were expected to install their own individual air-conditioners. In time, occupants of offices found that the air-conditioning was so cold that they put on jackets. Gradually the trend arose for the grander office workers (certainly the executives) to appear always in suits and ties. Some Western *hongs* (companies) even required their staff to wear suits all the time. Within the Colonial Secretariat, the CS (John Nicoll) insisted that anyone who entered his office should wear a jacket and tie. This could cause problems with some visitors who did not expect such protocol in a hot climate. Elsewhere in the Government, dress in the office was usually left to individual discretion. Many Chinese staff simply did not possess a jacket; most men wore a shirt (often white) and shorts or long trousers. Girls came in Western-style skirts or increasingly in trousers. Today, in summer, looking from above at a lunchtime crowd of office workers crowding the pavements in Central HK, one is immediately struck by the hundreds of white shirts, presumably churned out in huge numbers from textile factories in HK and China. In the immediate post-war years, smarter Chinese girls wore Chinese-style dresses with slits up the sides. Waitresses in restaurants and tea-houses always wore them. Male Shanghai tailors were usually considered the best source for Chinese dresses. The fashion died out, to the extent that, except in some restaurants, a Chinese dress is now hardly ever worn. Virtually all Chinese in HK now wear Western-style clothing, partly because it is mass-produced and cheaper.

In earlier post-war days, middle-aged and elderly Chinese women could sometimes be seen with a walking stick hobbling round on tiny bound feet. The practice happily died out post-war but women who had suffered this form of beauty treatment in previous years still struggled on. Although there were few reminders of the Japanese Occupation to be seen, some adults carried the legacy of malnutrition and vitamin-deficiency, in the form of white patches on their cheeks. We had an excellent amah for years with pockmarks of smallpox on her face. Similarly marked individuals who had survived the disease in China could be met from time to time. With the worldwide eradication of smallpox in recent years, there will hopefully be no more such pockmarks to be seen.

The biggest killer of Chinese in the ten to twenty years after the Pacific War was pulmonary tuberculosis, spread by overcrowded living conditions, lack of resistance resulting from poor diet, and the common habit of spitting. The drawnout clearing of the throat followed by the sound of the spit itself used to be described as the 'HK anthem'. It puzzled me where all the sputum came from (I could never produce so much), till it was explained to me that Chinese in those days were prone to nasal problems as well as TB. Dried sputum from a person with TB could reach an uninfected person. It took many years of publicity and enforcement to reduce the practice of spitting in public. Nowadays it is seldom met in HK. Treatment of TB used to involve six months in hospital, meaning that the victim's family meanwhile received no income, and his employer temporarily lost a worker. The Government was forced to take action to stop employers summarily dismissing employees who developed TB without giving them any paid sick leave.

Better housing, more jobs and income, an awareness of improved diet and, above all, more effective medicine (including ambulatory treatment, i.e. no in-patient treatment), reduced the incidence of TB enormously in later years.

Life in the DO's quarters at the Lookout, Tai Po Kau, was pleasant although cut off from the mainstream of social life in the urban areas. It could take the better part of an hour to drive on the narrow winding road to Kowloon, usually for shopping once a week at a *compradore* (a Portuguese word meaning a grocer) in Nathan Road which in those days was lined at its southern end by huge banyan trees. There was never any problem finding a car parking space between the trees. Nowadays no parking is allowed there; some of the trees have gone, others have had branches lopped to allow the safe passage of double-decker buses. The Chinese *compradore* was cheerful, friendly, and prepared to allow credit. This was helpful as my salary for my first two years of service amounted to $720 a month, insufficient to cover expenses and we were by no means extravagant. I learnt to pay bills from the electricity and telephone companies as a priority, because they would cut supplies if not paid on time; other bills would be paid as and when I could.

The water supply for the Lookout came free of charge by pipe from the all-year stream running through the Forestry Reserve at Tai Po Kau, about a mile from the house. Although the water was unfiltered, it was unpolluted and tasted good. It also served to fill the tiled swimming pool near the house. Standing in the pool one day beside the inlet pipe, I was delighted to notice a bewildered freshwater shrimp emerge from the pipe and swim round the pool.

Having hitherto taken little interest in gardening, I found that the possession of a garden stimulated me to learn about local plants and trees, leading in time to a deep interest in gardening and a love of making things grow. Situated north of the equator in the Tropic of Capricorn, HK is not a tropical country like Malaysia but has a distinct summer (when it is hot and wet) and a winter (when it is cooler and dry). It can at times be cold (down to 5°C) in winter. The result is that a wide range of plants can grow in HK, although tropical ones may not thrive. With heavy rain leaching nutrients out of the soil, the key to successful gardening in HK lies to some extent in continual improvement of the soil and pruning to lessen damage from storms. Trees seldom grow to any height in HK because they can be snapped off or uprooted by typhoons.

Chapter VII

In the summer of 1949, a typhoon (anglicised version of the Cantonese 'dai foong', meaning 'big wind') approached HK. As I grew to learn in later years, you could read the signs a day or two beforehand: leaden sky with grey-blue clouds, sultry oppressive atmosphere, sudden puffs of wind. Sometimes it could be a tropical storm approaching, other times a proper typhoon. People usually listened to their radio for the hourly weather bulletin as the storm approached, and made their preparations. The pattern evolved over many years was clearcut. When the storm approached within a certain distance of HK, the Royal Observatory (in Nathan Road, Kowloon) would hoist the No. 1 signal, and the radio would describe the storm's central wind speed, distance from HK, the speed with which it was travelling, its present course, and the time it would take to reach HK if it continued on its present course. Big ships in the harbour might cut short their stay and make off in good time to avoid rough seas. Airlines might alter schedules. Fishing vessels, lighters and harbour launches would make for the several typhoon shelters, packing tight inside there. Prudent residents would bring indoors all moveable objects (e.g. flowerpots) from outside. Windows would be firmly closed, likewise any louvred shutters. Shopkeepers ceased business and pulled down metal roller blinds over their glass shop fronts. Nos. 2-6 signals denoted the direction of the storm and its closer approach. By the time No. 7 was hoisted, the wind would be blowing hard and rain crashing down. No. 9 meant the storm was on you but few ever saw it, being more occupied with survival indoors.

Not every typhoon making for HK reached the territory with a direct hit. Sometimes it would change direction and merely brush past, with a middling blow: destructive perhaps but not catastrophic. (A typhoon in

HONG KONG THEN

October 1937 arrived with little or no warning, coincided with a high tide bringing a tidal surge, and killed tens of thousands, mostly fishermen). The modern development of radar, weather balloons, ship and aircraft reports make it easier to plot a typhoon's course, speed and intensity. In the thirty or so years after the Pacific War, typhoons in the season (May to September) were identified and named by the American weather bureau at the former Clark Field military base in the Philippines. They were always given girls' names. According to the cynics, this reflected the fickle female nature of the typhoons in frequently changing course. These days affirmative action seems to have resulted in the introduction of boys' names for typhoons. Indeed the word 'typhoon' is being replaced by 'cyclone', losing much of the charm of a traditional local word.

In the Lookout in that far-off summer, Margaret and I were not aware of the power of the storm. As the wind and rain increased, we closed doors and windows and wondered whether the glass would stand the strain. The sound of the wind rose to a scream on the windward side, and water was forced through the edges of the doors and windows. We embarked on what became a familiar drill in the dozen or so typhoons we experienced during our thirty-five years in HK, excluding milder but equally wet tropical storms. The worst of the typhoon might last several hours (too often at night time), during which we moved constantly, tightening door and window latches as they worked loose and mopping up the streams of water that poured in. If the wind seemed too strong, rooms on the windward side would be evacuated in case the windows blew in, with glass flying round lethally.

Great care had to be exercised in opening and closing doors inside the house, as wind pressure might force the door to slam, trapping your fingers. The force of the wind on one side of the building and the corresponding suck on the other side could cause multi-storey towers to sway alarmingly, up to one metre claimed some upper-storey residents. Living up the Peak in later years, a feature that always surprised me in big storms was the fact that the level of water in WC pedestals would move up and down, presumably as a result of air pressure in the sewer or even of movement of the sea at the sewer outlets hundreds of feet further down the hill. No one with any sense ventured out of doors, for fear of flying objects. Sheets of corrugated iron could slice through the air, taking your head off. Everything in the territory came to a standstill, often including the electricity. It was a wise precaution to have torches handy and stocks of tinned food to last a couple of days. When the wind speed reached 100 m.p.h., it could be really terrifying.

Although a typhoon would be moving in a certain direction, the wind near the centre would be revolving in a circle. This meant that, if there was a direct hit on HK, the wind would blow from one quarter until the centre reached the territory. There would then be a brief lull (the eye of the typhoon) before the wind rose again, blowing from the opposite quarter.

One of the biggest dangers from the rain brought by a typhoon or tropical storm was the number of landslips in the steeper parts of the territory. Over the years there were numerous tragedies from dislodged boulders, house collapse, flooding and blocks of flats carried away. Emergency services could be kept busy directly after a storm, saving life, restoring electricity and water, and clearing blocked roads and drains. Trees exposed to the wind would be stripped of leaves which could carpet roads an inch thick in a slippery mass. It was noticeable that, where a deciduous flowering tree had lost its leaves, a few weeks later it might flower again (twice in one year), presumably because its seasonal rhythm mistook the loss of leaves for the end of winter and therefore time to start flowering and putting on new leaves.

In 1949, the end of the storm at the Lookout found us weary and astonished at this unfamiliar natural phenomenon. Luckily we had suffered little damage, nor was there much when I toured round the district immediately afterwards. But, down in Tolo Harbour below the Lookout, there were vessels on the rocks, including one from the Chinese Maritime Customs which had sailed south seeking shelter from the storm.

Chapter VIII

During 1949, the Chinese Communist armies under Mao Tse Tung swept across China, driving the Nationalist forces before them. This naturally caused concern to the British Government which was unsure whether the Communists intended to take HK as well in their triumphal progress. The British garrison in HK was therefore increased, with most of the troops stationed in the NT. I was often called upon to accompany senior officers on visits of inspection to buildings and areas to judge their suitability as camps. Lieutenant General Sir Robert Mansergh (Commander British Forces, HK) called at the office one day where John Barrow and I briefed him on local conditions and the need for the Services to keep in close touch with the civil administration, so as to avoid incidents with villagers. For instance, I heard of a desire by a tank unit to run their tanks through growing paddy fields to find out whether tanks could manoeuvre in the soft soil or become bogged. This sort of thing had to be resisted, as being similar to the manner in which the Japanese forces rode roughshod over local interest during the Pacific War.

Until private land was requisitioned for the purpose or Crown land made available and permanent camps constructed, most units had to live temporarily in uncomfortable conditions, made worse by the summer heat, humidity and rain.

By arrangement, a unit of independent airborne Royal Engineers arrived one day and was placed temporarily in the new but unoccupied staff quarters of a cemetery. That evening Margaret and I drove round there and met the officers who were astonished to meet a European woman in what, as newcomers from the UK, they considered to be the back of a dangerous beyond. In one way or another, I got to meet most units and to understand their problems. The fact that I was a former army officer myself helped cement relations.

Once or twice a week, a group of young officers would come to the Lookout for drinks and dinner. Lieutenant Colonel Man, commanding a battalion of the Middlesex Regiment, stayed the weekend, glad to get away from the Mess. Two ratings from HMS *Amethyst* also spent a couple of nights with us. *Amethyst* at the time was anchored in Tide Cove below the Lookout. This was shortly after the incident in 1949 when *Amethyst* had sailed up the Yangtse river, been engaged by Communist Chinese artillery on the banks, and had eventually managed to escape downriver again. The ratings were charming and emptied the whisky bottle overnight.

In 1949, the main NT road ran from Kowloon up the eastern side of the NT past Tai Po to Fanling where it turned westwards to Castle Peak and then south back to Kowloon. From the military point of view, defence of the border was impracticable if the road north could be cut so easily by seaborne landings on the east and west sides. It was necessary to provide a road through the middle which happened to be mountainous but not impossible. In May 1949, shortly after I took over the job, I was required on a hot and steamy day to accompany the Director of Public Works and the roads engineer on a visit over the proposed route of such a central road. My job, with the assistance of George Roylance who knew more about it than I did, was to assess the amount of private land involved in the proposed route and the approximate cost of compensation if the private land was resumed. We clambered up the Lam Tsuen valley on traditional stone-paved paths, past terraced paddy fields already planted out, with occasional villages and barking dogs. It took hours to reach the pass at the top where the narrow ridge of Tai To Yan stretched off to the right and the steep sides of the mountain looked down at us on the left. The remains of age-old tea terraces could be seen on the grassy sides of the mountain on the left. From the pass, we continued on down to the plain of Bart Heung where vehicles awaited us. In the months and years to come, the Lam Kam Road was built, with gradients and width suitable for the movement of tank transporters. The HK Government built the road at its own expense on behalf of the Army which was then expected to take it over and be responsible thereafter for maintenance. At this stage, accountants came on the scene. The Army declined to be responsible for maintenance and, to emphasise its jurisdiction over the road, closed it to civilian traffic. A stalemate ensued. As District Officer, it was convenient and necessary for me to use the road, so I was issued with a military pass containing my photo. It so happened one day that Margaret wanted to go to Kam Tin for some purpose. I lent her my pass to go over the Lam Kam road where she was stopped by a Military Policeman disconcerted to find a European woman. She produced my pass which was duly inspected and she was waved on with 'thank you, madam', to her surprise since she did not look in the least bit like my photo.

In those days, the landward side of the road leading into Tai Po from Kowloon was lined with watercress beds. A dispute arose about ownership of some of the beds, and this fell to Donald Luddington to deal with in his capacity as Magistrate and Assistant Land Officer. He spent days trying to sort out the confused financial and leasing arrangements that many HK Chinese delight in producing. There is nothing like a legal tangle for sometimes lending an insight into business practice and attitudes of mind. Where Buddhist monks were involved in disputes, Donald was often surprised at their worldly ways and extreme views, unlike preconceived notions of peace and tranquillity.

At Christmas, a group of villagers appeared at the Lookout, bearing gifts. (This was in the days before the Independent Commission Against Corruption was set up, with its stern requirement that no civil servant should demand or receive any gift in respect of his duty.) It would have been churlish to refuse the fruit and eggs that the villagers had brought, but I was taken aback when a villager appeared with a live turkey under his arm. As we shook hands, the turkey escaped and ran off across the lawn, gobbling loudly, with everyone in hot pursuit.

Chapter IX

By late October 1949, the Communists sweeping down from the north had reached Canton (now renamed in English as Kwongchow), with the Nationalist Army in disarray. On 1 October Mao Tse Tung, from the balcony of the first building in the Forbidden City facing Tiananmen square in Beijing had proclaimed the establishment of the People's Republic of China. In HK, the question was whether the Communists would attempt to cross the border into HK. For days beforehand, refugees had flooded into the NT from China, crossing at the Lo Wu railway bridge or the Man Kam To road bridge. On the day that it was thought the Communists would reach the border, there was considerable nervousness in the NT, particularly amongst Europeans who had been POWs or internees of the Japanese during the Pacific War. They had no wish for a second dose. Larry Power, the European Police Inspector at Sha Tau Kok, told me later that he had personally taken a saw and cut off the flagpole (with the Union Standard) on the HK side of the border, so as to prevent the Communists running up their own flag if they crossed over. In the event, the Communists did not invade but remained hostile on their own side of the border.

For weeks before this, unarmed Nationalist troops in uniform had travelled by the KCR train from Canton or Shum Chun to Kowloon, where they bought up various goods which they then carried back into China. The story was that they sold the goods in China to supplement their pay. At any rate, it was nothing strange to see a Nationalist soldier shopping in Sheung Shui which in those days was a dirty mass of unregulated structures. Donald Luddington and I were invited one day, together with the NT Superintendent of Police, to attend a Chinese dinner in the evening in Sheung Shui. After the meal, we were walking back along an ill-lit lane to where our cars were parked, when a

Looking across the Lo Wu railway bridge from the Hong Kong side to the Chinese Communist side where Chinese Nationalist aircraft have set material alight (1949).

Material burning in China at the Lo Wu railway crossing, with a temporary Police post in a tent on the Hong Kong side.

Nationalist soldier suddenly appeared and accosted us in Mandarin (which none of us spoke). He held on to the policeman's arm. The Superintendent's wife started screaming; they had both been internees in HK during the Japanese Occupation. The prevailing state of nervousness about Communists and violence was such that the policeman drew his pistol, shoved it into the soldier's stomach, squeezed the trigger and swore loudly when the magazine dropped on to the ground. To a newcomer like myself, this seemed over-reaction and a lucky escape from an unnecessary killing. For all we knew, the soldier may have been hungry, destitute and begging for assistance.

On another occasion, a Nationalist soldier turned up at the Lookout and started to make a nuisance of himself, aggravated by no one understanding his Mandarin. He seemed mentally disturbed and had to be removed by the Police. Many of the refugees started to build wooden huts for themselves in the Tai Po district which had hitherto been completely free of these temporary structures. This gave rise to a new problem. Where the structure was on Crown land and in an unacceptable position, there were legal powers for its demolition. But it was a different matter on private land; there was at first little that could be done except to resume the land for breach of condition. Draconian measures were inappropriate for refugees who had nowhere to live. Many sought to plant on marginal land, digging wells to provide water. Again, this sometimes brought repercussions from local villagers complaining that the refugees were interrupting traditional water supplies. A new section of the District Office had to be set up to deal with temporary structures.

Pressure to develop land grew. John Barrow, the District Commissioner, gave approval for an area of rice fields at Luen Wo Hui to be converted to building status and be turned into a market town, which it is today. The opening ceremony for the new town took place on 21 January 1951, with a dramatic flourish of firecrackers that lasted for fully fifteen minutes. Each cracker, in red paper, is tied in a long string, one under the other and hoisted up on a bamboo pole. The noise is intended to drive away evil spirits and to ensure the prosperity of the project. Firecrackers and fireworks have since been banned in HK, to reduce the incidence of injuries and fires. Modern generations have probably never seen or heard the ear-splitting racket, the clouds of smoke, the smell of gunpowder, and the ground littered with red paper from the firing of a long string of crackers. In the course of the opening ceremony, Catherine Barrow enquired when Margaret's baby would be born, and was surprised when I said he had been born that very morning. I had already driven to Kowloon hospital and back before the ceremony.

John Barrow also approved the conversion of rice fields to building status on the seaward side of the road at Sha Tin. Hitherto these rice fields had borne a strain of red rice which local people claimed was held in such high esteem as to be placed in earlier generations before the Emperor himself in Peking. Looking at the massive skyscrapers and buildings that now line the road at Sha Tin, not to mention the racecourse, it is hard to visualise its original rural face, with rice fields stretching to the sea. Driving back to the Lookout from Kowloon, on a moonlit night, the sea was a wonderful sight with the reflection of the moon. On misty mornings in summer when the mountains on the eastern side of the inlet were all but hidden in the mist, it was not uncommon to find a dozen or more Chinese photographers with cameras on tripods snapping the dreamy landscape as the heat from the rising sun dispersed the mist and revealed the mountain peaks.

On the eastern side of Tide Cove stood the mountain of Ma On Shan, with an iron ore mine on its western flank. At the foot of the mountain at the sea was a pier for loading freighters with the iron ore which was stockpiled nearby in big brown heaps. Most of the miners were northern Chinese working in galleries below ground. I inspected the mine a few times, worried at its spread beyond the boundaries of the mining lease and its damage to vegetation, in particular the large wild azalea growing on the upper hill slopes.

Chapter X

The main work of the District Office, Tai Po, in 1949 and 1950 concerned the effect in the NT of the new Communist regime in China. This naturally included relations with the enlarged British garrison in the NT, but for me there was no contact with the People's Liberation Army on the other side of the border. My only brush occurred one day whilst walking along the border at Sha Tau Kok, watched closely by a Chinese soldier with a red-tasselled pistol who waved me back when I incautiously stepped beyond the boundary stones of 1898 (when HK took over the NT).

The Communists nevertheless carried on business with HK. Vehicle tyres, petrol in cans, and other goods were conveyed from HK across the border at Lo Wu and stockpiled on the other side. On a visit one day to Lo Wu, I was surprised to hear machine-gun fire overhead, followed by the noise of fighter-bombers flashing past from the HK side and firing at the stockpiles on the Chinese side of the border. From a prone position on the ground, I watched the Nationalist planes make repeated passes firing at the stockpile from which clouds of black smoke appeared. (The bottom of Taiwan, to which the Chinese Nationalists under Chiang Kai-shek had withdrawn after the loss of mainland China, lies opposite HK and involves a comparatively short flight.) These daylight aircraft attacks became commonplace until the stockpiles ceased to exist.

The outbreak of the Korean War in 1950 brought renewed anxiety about China's intentions for HK and the need for an increased British garrison. This rose to divisional strength, with more than one infantry battalion of Gurkhas. There were also newly-formed Gurkha units of engineers, signallers, drivers and other specialist arms; a change from the former policy of recruiting Gurkhas only in an infantry role.

The floods of Chinese refugees crossing the border into HK and the need for something to deter both them and any Chinese military incursion led in 1949-50 to the decision to build a fence along the land border of the NT. To assess the status of the land along the proposed line of the fence, George Roylance and I (armed with maps), together with a representative from the Architectural Office, walked the length of the border from Sha Tau Kok to Lo Wu. It took us several days, deciding whether the fence should detour inland to avoid deep ravines or should stick as closely as possible to the actual border. In practice, the fence was erected where it best suited the ground rather than the border itself which for part of the way ran down the centre of the Shum Chun river.

The Divisional Commander, Major General Geoffrey Evans, who had served in Burma in the Pacific War, wanted somewhere to live reasonably close to his headquarters in Sek Kong, in the flat central plain. I therefore took him round to various houses that might possibly be requisitioned; he liked none of them. He said he had heard of the White House at Tai Po, occupied at the time by a government colleague. Dismayed at the thought of being responsible for evicting a colleague, I brought the General round to the bottom of the steep path leading up to the house, explained that there was no vehicle road up to the house, and walked briskly ahead of him, knowing that he had a bad leg and limped. We had not progressed more than a few yards before the General said 'No, no. This won't do. I couldn't possibly walk up and down here in all weathers. Find something else.' So we did. Nothing like good tactics.

The White House was later occupied by Pat Dodge, a newly arrived cadet, who had taken over from Donald Luddington as Magistrate. Pat was a great cricketer and electrified the HK Cricket Club one day by scoring a century. (In those days, the Club's ground lay in Central District of HK on the site now occupied by Chater Garden.) Pat was also an amateur painter. Showing me his paintings one day, he failed to realise that the next one to be displayed depicted his wife nude on a leopard-skin rug. This was hurriedly covered up. One morning in the office, his amah appeared with a note from him to say that he had been to a party on the night before, was now suffering from a fit of the vapours, and was quite unable to attend the office. As an antidote for him, I took the opportunity of giving the amah a tin containing a small banded krait (poisonous snake) that I had killed that morning at the Lookout. Pat suffered a relapse.

South of HK and not forming part of the territory are a number of small islands on which the new Chinese Government lost no time in stationing garrisons, possibly to guard against Nationalist incursions. But the garrisons also fired from time to time at foreign vessels passing too close to them, presumably to emphasise the Chinese claim to territorial waters. When the Royal Navy was fired on, there were reports that the Navy responded by sailing by with guns loaded and trained on targets. At the first sight of a shoreward flash (before the sound and shell arrived), the Navy would fire back. Up the Peak in 1949-50, sounds of distant gunfire from south of HK were often heard, although this may also have been firing practice.

An area of land at Sha Tin alongside the inlet had been made available for a short air strip and accommodation for a flight of the AOP (Air Observation Patrol). Equipped with Lysander aircraft, these were Gunners whose role was to spot targets and control the fire of ground artillery. Naturally they made themselves familiar with the NT by flying all over it. Margaret and I got to know them well and were always thrilled to receive messages from them dropped in little weighted bags on the lawn of the Lookout.

Gaston de Martin and his wife were our nearest neighbours, about a quarter of a mile away, in a pre-war bungalow. Now retired, he had been the pre-war Deputy Director of Education; she was an enthusiastic gardener, ever ready with advice and cuttings. Gaston, on the other hand, took no interest in gardens. An elderly academic, he was a great talker and a fund of stories about pre-war life, including a tale about a NT resident who carried on a running fight with the Government over its failure to keep the Tai Po road in good repair. Shortly before the Governor was due to make a much-heralded trip round the NT, the resident parked his car across the narrow Tai Po road so as to block all traffic, locked it and departed home. Agitated official requests by

Formal gathering of the Heung Yee Kuk in Tai Po (New Territories) on the occasion of a visit by the Governor, Sir Alexander Grantham (with bow tie), in May 1949. I'm standing in the second row, sixth from the left.

telephone for him to remove the car were grudgingly acted upon in return for a guarantee that road repairs would be carried out at once. The resident then carried his war to the Post Office which in those days would deliver only letters, not parcels, in the NT. Addressees in the NT were then expected to go to Kowloon to collect their parcels. So the resident went to Kowloon, bought a fresh fish, wrapped it in a parcel addressed to himself in the NT, and posted it. He took no notice of the subsequent card from the Kowloon Post Office asking him to collect the parcel. He equally ignored the several subsequent requests. By the time the stench from the decomposing fish in the parcel was causing problems in the Kowloon Post Office, the resident had gained his point. The Post Office was not allowed to throw away mail, nor could it continue the stalemate. The Postmaster General capitulated and parcels were delivered to NT addresses.

Gaston himself was the source of another story. When Stanley Prison on HK island was first completed in the 1930s, there was the usual opening ceremony (without prisoners), followed by a visit of inspection of the premises by invited guests, including Gaston. Interested in the interior of a new cell, Gaston entered, not realising that the door was self-closing. He was apparently locked in for some while before he was discovered and released (cells being soundproof and the keys not readily available).

James Norman had been a member of the Prisons Department working pre-war in Stanley Prison. After the fall of HK in 1941, the Japanese locked up the prison staff in the Prison. Some time after the Pacific War ended, James eventually became Commissioner of Prisons and commented wryly that he must be the only Commissioner who had once been a prisoner in one of his own prisons.

When the mid-autumn festival came round at the full moon in September and it was still a hot wet summer month, it was hard to comprehend where the autumn was. The answer was that the Chinese calendar was geared to weather in north China; if south China produced a different climate, that was their misfortune. The festival was also the occasion for moon cakes which traditionally contained a whole duck's egg and what tasted like lard, making a heavy and unappetising mixture. Our amah presented us with half a dozen. Margaret and I started to eat one but, after a mouthful or two, felt under no compulsion to continue. We therefore gave it to the dog which spat it out the moment the amah came into the room.

A new village school which I had helped organise had recently been completed on the northern side of Starling Inlet, accessible by a dirt track. For the opening ceremony, local dignitaries had invited Sir Shouson Chow, a well-known figure in HK society. He turned out to be a short, smiling, elderly gentleman, dressed in a long gown and a long beard. In conversation with him after the ceremony, I found he was a fund of stories, ranging from hunting pre-war in Korea for bear and Siberian tiger to his early days in the USA. Travelling by stage coach in the west, he claimed to have been held up by some well-known bandit who demanded money. Sir Shouson apparently put on an act, got down on his knees and said, 'me, laundry boy – got no money'. This was enough to attract a kick and be told to get out of the way. Sir

Shouson was always good for an article in the publicity media. When in his nineties, he delighted in issuing challenges to a boxing match with any other person of the same age. As he was remarkably fit for his age, it was unlikely that he would ever be challenged. At the same time, he was an astute businessman in all sorts of fields including real estate. The residential area of Shouson Hill on the south side of HK was named after him.

Chapter XI

Living and working in the NT, Margaret and I seldom went to HK island, except occasionally to visit Mr and Mrs Cassidy. They would invite us to lunch in the restaurant (called The Grips) in the former Gloucester Hotel in Pedder Street. Having occasion one day to go into a jeweller's shop in the same street, we were addressed by the middle-aged European lady behind the counter in perfect English. She then turned to a European man with her and spoke to him in fluent French, breaking off to call out to her Chinese assistant in voluble Cantonese. The Cassidys immediately knew who I meant when I described the incident.

In the days when the European community in HK was comparatively small, most of them knew each other or at least had heard of each other, bearing in mind that the majority were long-term residents with travel to and from HK almost entirely by sea. The later trend towards short contracts for expatriates and travel by air meant a larger European community where it was not possible to know everyone. This was aggravated by the increasing tendency as the years passed for those in a particular field to circulate largely in that field. Those in shipping might keep to themselves, likewise the hospitality industry (hotels, restaurants), airlines, import/export, consular and government servants. Bankers tended latterly to have a hard time gastronomically, finding themselves lunching and dining with customers on most weekdays.

It was in sport that expatriates crossed the business boundary and got to know a wider cross-section of the community. Generally expatriates made friends amongst other expatriates, but as the years passed the circle widened to include Chinese, many of whom had travelled and were educated overseas. Chinese friends always spoke English to expatriates, although they might converse with each other in

Cantonese at a mixed gathering, switching to English on the approach of a European. Unless an expatriate was absolutely fluent in Cantonese and the only European in an otherwise Chinese group, attempts by Europeans to speak Cantonese on social occasions were not welcomed. Generally professional Chinese spoke far better English than the majority of Europeans spoke Cantonese. It was a different matter in relations with staff in Chinese shops and workers elsewhere. They might speak some English but lacked practice.

Entering a Chinese shop, I could often see a cloud passing over the face of the assistant who was perhaps wondering how, with his limited knowledge of English, he was going to manage. When I addressed him in Cantonese, his eyes would light up. Not all Chinese would react in this manner. On several occasions accompanied by a Chinese colleague on official duties, I would speak to a Chinese who was less educated and unfamiliar with Europeans. The Chinese would turn to my colleague and ask, 'What's this foreign devil saying?' My colleague would reply in the same words that I had used, with exactly the same tonal inflections. It was apparent that from the outset the questioner had been convinced in his mind that no European could speak Chinese and that therefore my Cantonese was not Cantonese at all but some sort of gibberish. It was the brain rather than the ears that had failed to register. There is nothing like a preconceived notion for misleading one.

The general practice amongst Chinese was to offer hospitality, not in the private home, but in a restaurant, perhaps in a private room. This was partly a matter of practicality, in that the home may not have the space, cooking facilities, or staff to provide for a table of ten persons (the social dining table usually sat ten). Traditionally, the host sat facing the doorway so that he could see and greet arriving guests. In banquet style, a formal Chinese meal might consist of twelve courses that traditionally started with small bits and pieces, moved on to soup, then to meat (fish, pork, beef, pigeon, poultry), shark's fin soup, fried rice, and a sweet dish.

Traditionally, the menu should contain something that swam, something that flew, and something that crawled. Whilst the shark's fin was being served, the host would normally drink a toast to his guests. If there were more than one table, the host would walk from table to table toasting the guests, holding the glass in one hand with the fingers of the other hand touching the bottom of the glass. In the early days, guests (usually all men) were served brandy or whisky, and were called upon to drink numerous toasts with cries of *'yum shing'*, meaning drink it all. It took me some time to discover, by watching other Chinese, that there was no need to swallow glasses full of brandy. You could get away with merely taking a sip and wrapping your hand round the glass so as to hide its contents.

Chinese hosts too often felt it their duty to make sure that their guests ate and drank more than they wanted. As regards food, it was commonplace for a host, on seeing a guest's bowl to be empty after he had finished a course, to fill it up again. It might be useless to protest, although possibly unacceptable to continue eating, knowing there were more courses to follow. Again, I learnt from example that it was sufficient to make a token effort of eating, leaving the rest in the bowl which would be removed between courses.

Over the years, Chinese wives began to appear at formal Chinese dinners, likewise European women. As a result, soft drinks were increasingly provided at dinners and the former emphasis on drinking spirits gradually diminished. Many felt that beer was a better accompaniment to a Chinese meal. One of the few Chinese who always provided a Western wine with a Chinese dinner was the late Teddy Lau Chan-kwok, head of the Yaumati Ferry Co, who served champagne at the splendid dinners in his private home.

The gradual switch from spirits to milder drinks at Chinese dinners reflected the dropping of the earlier local view that one drank (often to excess) in order to get drunk, not as a pleasant adjunct enjoyed for its therapeutic value and taken within one's capacity. To some extent, the switch also related to the need for those about to drive home to be below the legal limit for alcohol in the blood. The courts take an increasingly grim view of drink-driving. Many Chinese were reluctant to drink alcohol, because they complained that it made them red-faced, as blood rushed to their cheeks. All this was yet another instance of post-war changes in traditional Chinese attitudes in HK. It emphasised the fact that Chinese custom might be relevant only to the time it was recorded and might not necessarily apply at a later date.

But one Chinese custom that still endures is the practice of giving and receiving with both hands. This was important for European Government officials (and their wives) to appreciate on the several occasions on which they were called upon to hand out certificates or articles to Chinese members of the public. Good manners required the use of both hands, not one hand in the customary European manner.

Chapter XII

At the Cassidy's one day in 1950, we met their son, Hugh, who had been at school and at Oxford with me. He had later joined the Malayan Civil Service which had sent him, together with a group of other MCS men, on a course to Macao to learn Cantonese. Margaret and I therefore visited them there. Macao was technically not a Portuguese colony but a province of Portugal, sending two representatives to the Portuguese parliament. Situated some 40 miles west of HK on the other side of the estuary of the Pearl river leading up to Canton (now Kwongchow), it was a quiet charming backwater and a complete contrast to the hustle and bustle of HK. Traffic was so scarce that you could safely cross a road without looking both ways. Itinerant hawkers plied their wares in the traditional manner, with the knife-grinder clicking his scissors, the pots and pans man banging a tin, and the vegetable man making his peculiar cry. Housewives and amahs could at once recognise the cries and rush out to purchase. There was no roar of traffic and no sound of aircraft. People walked or rode in rickshaws. The Post Office sold stamps not only for Macao but also for all other Portuguese territories, together with a helpful map to show where they were.

Many HK residents spent weekends in Macao, enjoying the atmosphere, Portuguese meals (largely African chicken), Portuguese red wine (in big wickerwork-covered bottles), or vinho verde, and a flutter at the casino which in those early days was situated in the former Central Hotel. A favourite game was fan tan, consisting of a heap of small counters (looking like trouser buttons) that a croupier divided into groups of four. Punters then bet on whether the heap would be reduced finally to one, two, three or four counters. I remember seeing one punter throw down a red HK $100 note, which was quite a lot of money then, and then walk off in disgust part of the way through the croupier's process of dividing. The punter's practised eye had presumably worked out the final counters ahead and he realised he had lost. He was no doubt also cutting a dash in front of the other, less experienced punters.

Margaret and I went one day with the Malayan cadets on an expedition by ferry to the small islands of Kau Lau Wan and Taipei which were part of Macao and lay a few miles south. The ferry turned out to be a launch, with the passengers sitting on the roof. We set off through the shallow brown waters surrounding Macao. (On the larger ferry from HK, the usual colour of the sea had changed to a muddy brown as we reached the mouth of the Pearl river). It was low tide and we had not gone far before the launch stuck on a sandbank. A member of the crew jumped overboard up to his waist and, with much shouting and heaving, managed to free the vessel which took off for a deeper channel, leaving the crewman yelling and waving frantically astern. The captain was apparently reluctant to return in case the vessel grounded again, so we hung about whilst the unfortunate crewman waded towards us, disappearing at intervals into unexpected potholes.

The only beach with sand in Macao from which one could swim was Hak Sha (literally black sand) on Kau Lau Wan, with comparatively clear water. Nowadays, not only are these two islands joined to Macao by causeway and road, but an airfield has been constructed there too. In the process of making Macao more like HK with industry, vehicles and multi-storey blocks, the territory has sadly lost much of its charm.

Walking one day, we met a squad of black Portuguese troops (from Angola or Mozambique) dressed in full equipment, rifles and helmets, but without boots, and apparently on a route march. The Portuguese sergeant in charge wore no equipment and rode in the rear on a bicycle from which he dismounted as the squad reached a small hill. Giving a loud whistle to draw his attention, he handed over the bicycle to one of the Africans to push up the hill whilst he himself strolled along with his hands in his pockets. Rank has its privileges.

Some years later, whilst posted to the Urban Services Department, I had suggested to the Government that a group of senior USD officers

A group of cadets for the Malayan Civil Service (I'm wearing dark glasses on the right) on board a local ferry in Macau in 1950, bound for Kau Lau Wan.

The gateway in Macau leading into China (I'm second from the right), 1950.

should visit Macao and discuss operational problems with our opposite numbers there to see if they could suggest better ways of doing things. This was agreed and we duly visited. My particular interest lay in public toilets. On my enquiry whether I could look at some, our hosts directed the conversation elsewhere and I began to realise that this was an area best left unvisited. Our opposite numbers were charming and most hospitable, taking us to parts of the territory not normally open to tourists. The small museum contained a splendid collection of watercolours painted during the Pacific War by a White Russian, and depicting scenes of HK and Macau. On one occasion, we had arranged to meet our hosts at a particular time. Our HK group arrived in good time before the appointed hour. As a public clock struck the time, our hosts arrived beaming all over. 'Ah, we arrive in English time.' On our looking puzzled, they explained that Portuguese rated punctuality as a particularly English habit.

At the conclusion of the Russian Revolution in 1917, numbers of White Russians opposed to the new regime travelled eastwards to Vladivostok and found their way to Manchuria, many settling in Harbin, Shanghai and HK. Even post-war, the Russian community in HK was originally quite large in all sorts of activities, including horse racing. As the years passed, the community dwindled. Many migrated to the USA, Canada and Australia. But there were still sizeable numbers in China, particularly farming communities in Manchuria. It was in the 1950s that China pursued a policy of ethnic cleansing by ridding itself of all permanent resident Europeans. These included the Russians and foreign missionaries, deported to HK. Weary and bewildered, they arrived in trainloads at the railway terminus in Kowloon.

Whereas the missionaries were taken care of by officials of their own denominations, the Russians had no one to help but the UN High Commission for Refugees and the HK Government which placed them in temporary accommodation pending their acceptance as migrants to various countries. For weeks and months, the Russians eked out an unhappy existence in unfamiliar surroundings with little or no money. Big, bearded, blond men wearing thick clothing appropriate for the colder weather of northern China could be seen wandering uncomfortably round HK, accompanied by their womenfolk in long pinafore dresses from wrist to ankle and scarves tied round their heads. A group of their young men then hired themselves out as labourers to Chinese contractors engaged on road works. For weeks, it was commonplace to see these men working in trenches at the side of the road, often at a faster rate than the smaller and less burly Chinese labourers. Knots of curious Chinese passers-by would stop and comment on the unusual sight of Europeans working as coolies. But it gave the Russians something to do and provided a welcome source of income.

In due course, the last of these Russians was accepted elsewhere as a migrant, to lead a different life. (A few years later, Miss Australia turned out to be one of these Russian migrants.) HK now has hardly any Russians left.

In the same manner, the former large Portuguese community in HK has dwindled, with few of the old long-established families left. The remainder have migrated. This causes problems, with institutions for the Portuguese community like the Club Lusitano and the sporting clubs which find it hard to keep going with so few members.

It may come as a surprise to learn of the other permanent minority communities in HK, such as the Indian, Pakistani and Armenian. The Indians, many of whom have lived in HK for generations, are partly in the clothing business and have played a leading part in HK affairs. The Pakistanis tend to fill minor posts such as watchmen and doorkeepers; Armenians have been successful businessmen in the Far East for a century or so. Eurasians of mixed heritage have been present since HK became a colony. Usually speaking fluent Cantonese and English, they have been of great use in supervisory positions or in business where their knowledge of local conditions is a considerable asset.

There were many European missionaries in HK, both Roman Catholic and Protestant, working largely amongst the Chinese population in various fields, such as education, medicine and social welfare. To avoid the impression that they were a privileged caste, many of the missionaries lived in the Chinese style, eating Chinese food and, of course, speaking Cantonese. Pre-war, Italian priests had been well to the fore, particularly amongst the Hakka round Mirs Bay and Bias Bay to the east of HK. These dedicated people often lived lonely lives, seldom speaking their own tongue and visiting their homeland only at long intervals.

Chapter XIII

In the middle of 1950, I was posted temporarily to the Secretariat for Chinese Affairs (SCA) in the former Fire Brigade Building, in response to a cry for help. In practice, I found little or nothing to do and wondered what the fuss was about. For a month, I largely occupied myself learning the ways of Chinese family life, in the process of handling family cases. Where a Chinese couple were not getting on with each other, they might apply to the SCA to mediate and, if necessary, arrange their separation. It was a measure of the respect for the integrity and good reputation of the SCA that the couple were prepared to air their differences before a stranger and a European at that. Although I could follow much of what was said, provided the regional accent was not too pronounced, I always worked through an interpreter, partly because he could guide me with unfamiliar habits and customs. An essential first step in family cases was to discover whether the parties were properly married under Chinese custom or cohabiting under some lesser bond (few in those days were married in registry offices, although it is now the normal practice as a means of ensuring enforceable legal protection). A *kit fat* marriage was the traditional form of marriage and assumed that the parties were single and unmarried beforehand. Important features were exchange of horoscopes by the respective families, negotiations by a go-between, signing of the red paper of betrothal, exchange of presents, bridal chair (or decorated taxi) from the bride's home to her groom's, feast at groom's house to announce the marriage. It was not usual to omit any of these details, of which the red paper was perhaps the most important. A *tin fong* marriage was again a customary one, occurring where one of the parties to a *kit fat* marriage had died or was formally divorced. The surviving spouse could subsequently contract another formal marriage, with all the force of a *kit fat* marriage.

A *chip sz* or concubine had a definite status and could be formally taken on in addition to a customary wife, although usually with the wife's consent. The purpose of a concubine was generally to provide the sons that the *kit fat* wife had failed to produce (only males could take part in ancestor worship). But sometimes a concubine's prime duty was to assume the marital duties that an older *kit fat* wife was glad to delegate. In every case, as the senior, the *kit fat* wife ruled the roost. More prudent husbands tended to run separate households for wife and concubine, so as to avoid friction.

Mistresses were usually taken on without the knowledge of the wife and lacked any form of protection if discarded. Appendix A describes in greater detail the various aspects of Chinese custom that I came across in the course of my duties as District Officer. Few of these customs are likely to be practised today.

It was commonplace in many family cases for the girl to complain of assault by the man, and she would offer evidence by pulling up a sleeve or trouser leg to display bruises or cuts. Sometimes tempers would become heated, with the parties almost coming to blows. In one case, a tiresome girl demanded all sorts of compensation, threatening suicide if she failed to receive it. Tired of this rhetoric, I told her to get on with the suicide and stop wasting my time. At that, she leapt off her chair, raced to the window, and was starting to clamber out before the interpreter and I managed to grab her legs and pull her back. It was possibly more a defiant gesture than a serious attempt, but it taught me to be more careful. In another case, I was embarrassed to find the husband to be a European fireman from the Fire Brigade, with a disgruntled Chinese wife. At the end of a month, I was glad to be released from the SCA to return to the comparative quiet of the District Office, Tai Po, for my second summer in HK.

It may be difficult in these days of air-conditioned HK to imagine the continuing discomfort of the summer heat and humidity of an earlier age. Offices usually had ceiling fans but, even so, papers would stick to your elbows, sweat would drip, and the chair could attach itself to the seat of your trousers. Sleep did not come easily in the stifling heat at night when there was no breeze. Activity out of doors could be worse. Prickly heat, particularly amongst children, was a common complaint for Europeans, with itchy rashes in the fold of the elbow, round the neck, or in the groin. Watson's, the leading Western-style chemist, produced a prickly heat cream which was a white oily ointment that was usually effective but could make a mess of one's clothes.

The stream that ran down through the Tai Po Kau forestry reserve and that supplied water to the Lookout was a favourite spot for picnics. A whole school was enjoying a picnic there one summer's day amongst the boulders and thick tree-cover lining the banks when there must have been a sudden storm high up on Grassy Hill at the head of the stream. The first that the schoolchildren and teachers knew of this was when, with a great roar, a wall of water rounded a bend and swept through the picnickers, drowning ten or more. A week or two later, as I lay awake sleepless on a hot and airless night, I was surprised to hear screams and shouts from the direction of the stream. Locals had earlier reported hearing these anguished cries from what was described as the ghosts of those drowned. I was not mistaken in what I heard and have no reason to doubt the origin of the cries.

In 1951, I was posted to the Secretariat in HK as an assistant secretary in the Establishment Branch, dealing with pay, pensions, leave and suchlike. I disliked the work which meant that I had no contact with the public, but I began to learn the real job of paperwork. It was a requirement then that, if a head or deputy head of a department was away sick, a report should be made to the Establishment Branch, with an indication of what was wrong with the officer and when he was likely to return to duty. There was an obvious need for the Colonial Secretary to be kept informed of who was running the particular department. A report came one day from the Fire Brigade to say that its deputy head was away sick, but there was nothing to say what he was suffering from and when he might be back to duty. So I telephoned Mr Gorman, the Chief Officer, Fire Brigade, a colourful character. Gorman said he was not too clear but he thought his deputy had appendicitis. I therefore rang the hospital and learnt that the deputy was languishing with bronchitis. On my reporting this to Gorman, he replied, 'I knew it was something wrong with his stomach.' Some years later, I myself developed appendicitis. My appendix was removed in Kowloon Hospital by Dr Philip Mao who I later got to know well in quite a different capacity. Whilst I was convalescing later in the general ward, a European Fire Brigade officer was brought in, suffering from inhalation of toxic fumes. That evening Gorman came to visit him. The officer explained that he had been called out to deal with a drum leaking gas. Without an oxygen mask, he had apparently put his head over the top of the drum to look inside and had been overcome by fumes. Gorman was furious at this stupidity and at the top of his voice told the officer what an idiot he was and that he would not stay long in his job if he did that sort of thing again. The officer was left unhappy and crestfallen. To my amazement, he calmed his nerves by smoking a cigarette.

The Secretariat building in 1951 was a pre-war two-storey brick structure with polished teak floors and dated from the nineteenth century. The floorboards had shrunk over the years and at one point on the lower floor you could see up to the next floor. It was a stately building with a splendid curved wooden staircase more in keeping with something in a baronial mansion. But of course it was now too small and moves were afoot to replace it with larger offices.

A report came one day that Malcolm Macdonald, Secretary General for South-East Asia, was arriving from Singapore and would deliver a speech to members of the Executive and Legislative Councils in the Council Chamber on the first floor of the Secretariat. Malcolm Macdonald had an enviable reputation as politician and administrator, and I determined to hear him. Making my way through the Press reporters and agitators gathered outside, I slipped in at the back and listened to a brilliant exposition of the political situation in the Far East. He was a short toothy man, self-assured and articulate. Emerging afterwards, I saw Kennedy-Skipton trying to buttonhole Macdonald but fended off by Police and officials. Kennedy-Skipton was known as an activist pushing impossible political causes. Tall, thin, elderly and ill-dressed, he was well known in HK. As a senior member of the

Witnessing the oath-taking at a meeting of a newly elected Rural Committee in the New Territories (1951).

Government, he had been the pre-war head of the Sanitary Board at the time of the outbreak of the Pacific War. On the strength of an Irish passport, he had avoided internment by the Japanese and was accused post-war of having collaborated with them. He had unsuccessfully challenged his subsequent dismissal from the Colonial Service. But instead of departing quietly from HK, he had continued to live there, in what can be described as reduced circumstances, agitating on behalf of strange political causes and, despite his age, taking part with some success in long-distance races.

When I was DO in Tai Po, I had been made a Justice of the Peace, to allow me to hear statutory declarations. In HK, a JP was not required to sit on the bench or undertake any judicial duties; these were performed by professional magistrates. Instead, JPs were expected to carry out visits of inspection once a quarter to various government and private institutions. For a time, I was allocated visits to prisons, including the Old Bailey Prison for prisoners on remand. On a number of occasions there, I met a European prisoner named Johnson who had been sentenced to a lengthy term of imprisonment at the conclusion of the Pacific War for collaboration with the Japanese. Exceptionally, he was held in the remand prison instead of Stanley Prison where he had been beaten up by other prisoners incensed by his crime.

The procedure for these visits began with a letter from the Secretariat detailing the institution to be visited, the period during which the visit should be made, and the other JP who would accompany me. It was the practice for these visits to be made by two JPs: one being a Government official, and the other a private individual. The institutions ranged from prisons, to hospitals, clinics and social welfare establishments. The object of the visits was to check that everything was in order and that no irregularities were apparent. The JPs were also expected to hear any complaints from prisoners or inmates. At the end of the visit, the JPs would comment in the JPs' book which would be brought to the notice of the head of the government department concerned. The system worked well as a means of ensuring that the work in the institutions was properly performed and that no obvious irregularity occurred behind closed doors. Admittedly, staff in the institutions were warned of the coming visit but the system nonetheless acted as a deterrent to obvious abuses.

It was the convention that, in arranging the visit with his other JP, the official JP would provide transport in the form of a government car. On one occasion, I was required to visit a prison in the NT with the head of the Bank of China in HK (the official bank for China). When I spoke to him, he insisted that we could travel in his car. I agreed and was surprised to discover that it was a comfortable Rolls Royce with a liveried chauffeur. In the course of the journey, I remarked that I had heard that air-conditioning was not good in Rolls Royces. 'Oh, no,' said the banker, 'it's perfectly adequate in both my Rolls Royces.'

Chapter XIV

In those days, a tour of duty for expatriate government servants lasted four years followed by leave of seven months. Since travel to and from leave (usually spent in the UK) meant a sea voyage of one month in each direction by a regular P & O passenger liner, there was a total absence from HK of nine months. This was quite a long time but reckoned to be the minimum for an expatriate to recover his health after the arduous tropics and to renew ties with friends and relatives. In keeping with the usual practice, Margaret had preceded me with our son to Western Australia to see her parents, and would then continue by sea to England to meet me.

Travelling by sea first class on the P & O was a comfortable existence, with excellent meals, never-ending deck games, shore excursions at Singapore, Penang, Colombo, Bombay, Aden, Port Said and Marseille before arriving in Tilbury. A HK matron with years of experience in the Far East (one of the Old China Hands) explained to me that wives who knew the ropes played hard (golf, tennis, parties) and also worked hard (looking after the household and their family, and helping with local charities). She remarked that, on the outward voyage from England, by the end of the first week when the ship neared Gibraltar, passengers had got to know each other and any budding romances were on their way; it was the tradition that the romance ended when the passengers left the ship at the conclusion of the voyage. For passengers with a roving eye, the voyage could be a splendid interlude.

In the weeks before embarking on leave, many government officials and business expatriates suffered from a condition known as boat-happy. Dreamy, forgetful and unreliable, they would count the days to departure, when a crowd of friends would gather on board with much drinking and toasting, to wish the lucky person bon voyage. Bells would ring and loudspeaker announcements came at departure time to get the guests ashore. It was not always easy to winkle out the last reluctant guest. In later years when tours were much shorter and travel was usually by air rather than by sea, boat-happiness became almost a thing of the past.

Not all boat passengers wanted to play deck games or watch never-changing seascapes. Some were uninterested in the occasional flying fish that landed on the deck or the schools of porpoise that played round the bow. Even the daily sweepstake to guess the distance travelled in the current 24 hours could pall. Too often, their escape was to the bar. One fat man with a red nose (who was an habitué at the bar) was encouraged one day when another couple remarked that they had just seen a rat scuttling along a companionway. The fat man then admitted that he, too, had seen a rat two days earlier but had not dared tell anyone.

Leave of seven months in the UK meant that, unless you intended to spend the whole time with relatives, it was necessary to lease accommodation. I was always surprised at one or two colleagues who would spend their entire leave staying with a succession of friends, with constant packing and telephoning to arrange the next port of call. In our case, we rented a two-storey house in Bethersden in Kent for our leave which began in the winter in early 1953 when there was a tidal surge in the North Sea, inundating parts of eastern Britain and western Europe. When my heavy luggage eventually arrived, having been passed by Customs in the goods shed at Tilbury, it proved to be wet on the outside and even wetter inside. We bought a new car which I test-drove in London down Park Lane, with a current arrangement whereby at the end of the leave the car was shipped to HK.

In the middle of 1953 came the Coronation of Queen Elizabeth II. I had secured tickets from the Colonial Office for Margaret and myself to watch the procession from stands in the Mall. Unusually it was a cold, wet day in June as we watched a string of closed carriages, troops and horses, doing our best to try to identify the various dignitaries passing by. Most had enclosed themselves in their carriages to keep out the miserable weather. Not so the giant Queen Salote of Tonga who, despite the rain, left her carriage open, waving massive arms to the cheers of the crowd and beaming all over. The King of Malaysia who shared her carriage looked far from happy, crouched uncomfortably with a rug over his knees and not a smile anywhere.

Our neighbour on the stand was Humphrey Crutwell, a pre-war cadet from HK whom I had briefly met but did not know. He too sat sadly in the rain, fortifying himself from time to time with sips from a Dettol bottle which presumably contained spirits and not Dettol.

Our leave came to an end and we embarked once more on a P & O ship. A fellow passenger proved to be the Sultan of Johore, accompanied by an official from the Malayan Civil Service and a Malay bodyguard who appeared to spend the night in the passageway outside the Sultan's cabin. On hearing that Margaret was Australian, the Sultan remarked that he had travelled by camel across Australia and knew the country well. He was a big tall man with tattooing on his forearms. His wife, a Romanian, looked sad but came to life brilliantly when dancing the Lancers with the MCS official at the ship's ball. Her small daughter was the same age as my son who spent most of the voyage playing with her. On one occasion, the Sultan remarked that a certain date was the happiest occasion of his life, because that was the day when his second divorce was completed. In my presence one day, he invited Margaret to have a drink with him in the bar; I was clearly not invited. Determined to play chaperone, I turned up in the bar too, and read a book in the far corner. At Singapore, the Sultan and family departed with a Police escort in an official car bound for Johore. As the MCS official explained to me, the Police escort was really to protect the Sultan if he should be attacked en route. I had not been aware that the Sultan was suspected of collaborating with the Japanese during the Pacific War and was understandably disliked.

Chapter XV

Returning to HK after nine months' absence made us feel almost like strangers. It took time to acclimatise ourselves again, for me to learn to renew concentration for eight hours a day, and to brush up my Cantonese. This time I was posted as District Officer, Yuen Long, on the western side of the NT. The job also included the duties of Police Court Magistrate (sitting on three days a week), Assistant Land Officer dealing with land disputes, and Magistrate of a Small Debts Court. The administrative work was much the same as it had been in Tai Po. The District Office, at the top of a hill on the western outskirts of the market town of Yuen Long, consisted of a two-storey pre-war building with the court and offices for the public on the ground floor and other non-public offices such as accounts and land registry on the upper floor. The building was fly-screened with ceiling fans, reasonably cool in summer and filled with the cries of black-necked starlings from the neighbouring hillside.

Court cases consisted partly of serious criminal cases to be remanded for trial by a judge in Kowloon, traffic offences and other minor misdemeanours. In common with my colleague in Tai Po, my powers were limited to awarding six months' imprisonment or a fine of $5,000. Having a degree in law from Oxford, I was not worried by the legal side of things, but not entirely sure on procedure and evidence, despite having passed the examination in criminal law and Cantonese required of all new cadet officers towards the end of my first tour. Cadets served on probation for their first three years. If they passed their examinations and were otherwise considered satisfactory, they were confirmed to the permanent and pensionable establishment. Over the years, there were a few sent packing at the end of their third year. Membership of the Administrative Service was not a sinecure.

I quite enjoyed my five months as a magistrate, although it did have its awkward moments. A Gurkha driver was charged with careless driving of a military vehicle and, from the evidence given by a Police Inspector, was clearly at fault. He had pleaded guilty and had nothing to say. When I said, 'The court finds you guilty and fines you . . .', a Gurkha officer leapt up from the back of the court and said, 'You haven't heard me yet. I'm the officer here to plead in mitigation.' 'Oh, all right,' I said, 'go ahead, but it won't make any difference to the verdict.' Possibly not in the best legal tradition but, although justice may have seemed somewhat rough and ready, the right answer was usually reached. At any rate, I never had any appeal against my verdicts. I had some sympathy with Gurkha drivers. Up till post-war, Gurkha soldiers had always served as infantry. Then it was decided to form other Gurkha branches such as engineers, transport, electrical and mechanical. As Gurkha officers explained, recruits came from a country which at that stage had few roads and fewer vehicles. Many recruits had never worn leather boots and were unfamiliar with traffic. But sympathy had its limits. The overriding view was that drivers should not be let loose on public roads with a lethal machine like a vehicle unless they were reasonably competent at driving.

There were a number of soldiers charged at times with traffic offences. The Army was still at divisional strength, with the bulk of troops stationed in the NT. On one occasion, a cocky British soldier driving a jeep was charged with pulling out from behind another vehicle (with the intention of overtaking) and colliding with an oncoming vehicle. He pleaded not guilty and produced a string of flimsy stories intended to confuse me, possibly in the belief that a civilian in distant parts was slow on the uptake. Irritated at his wasting my time, I demonstrated with objects on my desk that he was clearly travelling too close to the vehicle in front and, since the jeep was left-hand drive (not mentioned in the evidence but known to me from my military experience), he had been forced to pull out to the right of the road before he could see ahead whether the way was clear to overtake. But the way was not clear and a collision occurred. If the jeep had been further back from the vehicle in front, there would have been enough time for the soldier to return to his own side of the road. 'Guilty, fined $X.' The soldier looked crestfallen and likewise his officer.

Another soldier was charged with evading a taxi fare and pointing a rifle at the taxi driver to force him to go away. The soldier had taken the taxi from Yuen Long to his army camp, had got out of the taxi and run away without paying, with the taxi driver in hot pursuit. The soldier dashed into the guard-room, snatched up a rifle, and aimed it at the taxi driver who prudently retired and poured out his complaint at the local Police Station. I found the soldier guilty and fined him. When the court sitting finished, the European Police Inspector who had prosecuted met me in the passageway and politely emphasised that pointing a firearm at a person deserved a heavier sentence than I had imposed. I took his point and ordered a review. When a day or two later the soldier reappeared in court, he looked unhappy and was even more so when I sentenced him to a term of imprisonment.

In those days, the Salvation Army ran a remand home in Castle Peak for juvenile delinquents. The building was apparently two-storey with the Salvation Army captain and his wife (both Europeans) occupying the upper floor which they barricaded off at night time, because a teenage lad on the ground floor terrorised everyone else and made a practice of breaking out, committing offences outside, then returning to the free living at the remand home. When I found him guilty of the offences, I was in a quandary about the sentence. Because he was a juvenile, he could not be sent to an adult prison. There was no point in fining him, since he had no money, and there was no point in adding to his period in the remand home since he would probably continue to break out and commit offences. Adjourning the court and checking my powers in the Ordinance, I consulted the Police Inspector who saw no problem about the course of action I proposed. Returning to court, I sentenced the lad to half a dozen strokes of the birch. Legally this had to be done in the same premises as the court. So we waited till 5.30 p.m., by which time the District Office staff had departed home. The delinquent was brought in, bent over a table with his trousers down and his wrists and ankles held by Constables. A sturdy Police Sergeant then laid into him with a rattan cane, ignoring the screams of anguish. There was no further trouble in the remand home.

This was the period of the Korean War in which China to all intents and purposes was a party. The United Nations had applied an embargo on the sale or transfer of military equipment to China. This gave rise to attempts to smuggle material from HK into China, either by boat or across the land border. A case came up in court where a Revenue party in HK had caught several people in the act of smuggling large quantities of embargoed material. The Revenue Inspector prosecuting gave his evidence, clearly delighted at making such a huge seizure. To his obvious dismay, I found the accused not guilty, saying, 'At no stage did you show the court that the material seized was a prohibited export.' It pained me to do this when it was only too obvious that the accused were as guilty as could be, but with the possibility of a successful appeal it was wiser to stick to the law.

Stripped to the waist, on a hot day at the weekend, I was gardening in the DO's quarters at 'Dunrose' in Castle Peak when a Police van drove up and a sergeant sought my signature on a warrant to commit a villager to 14 days' observation in a mental hospital. His fellow villagers had asked for Police assistance to get rid of the man because of his disruptive and irrational behaviour. Before signing, I thought I had better have a look at the villager and satisfy myself that he appeared unbalanced. So I walked over to the van from which there came the sound of banging and hammering, and looked in through the barred window. A contorted face glared at me and spat. I went off to sign at once. A few days later, I received a memorandum from the Medical Department signed 'P.M. Yap, Psychiatric Specialist', saying in effect 'if you are the Mr Wilson who signed the committal warrant, you signed in the wrong place and it appears that you have committed yourself. When do you wish to come in? We will try to have a room ready for you.' It so happened that I knew Dr Yap and later got to know him well. We had been contemporaries at Oxford, although we never met there. Sadly, he died unexpectedly a few years afterwards.

There was some embarrassment at the court sitting after Chinese New Year when a group of villagers, including the chairman of the

75

Rural Committee, from San Tin near Deep Bay was charged with illegal gambling. The second day of the New Year was traditionally the day to stay indoors and, for men, to gamble. Hitherto the Police may have turned a blind eye to the practice but, on this occasion, they had pounced. I fined the villagers a token sum and confiscated the gambling paraphernalia which included a brass cube containing smaller cubes. This took my fancy. Afterwards I asked the Police Inspector what would happen to the cubes. 'We'll destroy them,' he said, but was happy enough to give them to me on my promising not to gamble. When I retired from HK, I presented them to the Museum of History which was delighted to receive these relics of a traditional pastime. (Because of its serious social consequences, gambling has for many years been banned in HK. You go to Macao if you want to gamble.)

I had sat only five months as a magistrate when it was decided that the good old days of expecting a District Officer to double up as magistrate must give way to a properly qualified member of the judiciary. It was time to replace an amateur by a professional. This turned out to be an Australian who clearly took a poor view of how things had hitherto been managed and was resolved to put matters on what he considered to be a proper footing. It was not long before I began to receive complaints from disgruntled motorists, both local ones and those from the urban areas. The general tone was: 'When you were magistrate, we always pleaded guilty and knew what the standard fine would be. So we had the money ready and could get away back to our business with a minimal loss of time. But this new magistrate takes far too long, won't accept guilty pleas but expects us to waste time by coming all the way back to Yuen Long to argue that we weren't guilty. We want more justice, less law.' Sadly there was nothing I could do about it.

Pat Dodge, my fellow DO Magistrate in Tai Po, was relieved of his magisterial duties at the same time as myself. He died some years ago, leaving me as the final District Officer to have served as a magistrate in the NT. Other surviving cadets served in earlier days as magistrates in other colonial territories.

Chapter XVI

It was in the 1950s and 1960s that numerous cadets transferred to HK from other colonies that had reached independence. They slotted into the HK order of seniority according to their years of service elsewhere. This put some local noses out of joint, complaining that these newcomers knew nothing about HK, were not required to learn Cantonese if over the age of 35, and should be placed at the bottom of the list irrespective of seniority elsewhere. I was not popular for remarking that, on the contrary, these newcomers brought fresh ideas, wider experience, and an antidote to any complacency on the part of Old China Hands. Austin Coates used to say, without bitterness, that he had arrived in HK as No. 15 in the seniority list but, on transfer to Sarawak a few years later, found himself at No. 29 as a result of imported cadets. Gradually the complaints died away, and the newcomers proved themselves loyal and efficient servants of HK, to the extent that years later it was sometimes difficult to remember whether X had served all his time in HK or had transferred there from elsewhere.

On my colonial training course in 1947-8, consisting of two terms, one at Oxford and one at the London School of Economics, the majority of us were destined for territories in Africa or Malaya. We were mostly wartime ex-Servicemen, impatient to be done with lectures and to get on with the job in our respective territories. At Oxford, one of our number, a humourless young man who tried to press his Communist views on lecturers, ceased to appear one day and was presumed to have been quietly sacked. An amiable African on the course said he found the content unappealing and dropped out.

The vast majority of us (and we numbered over 100 lads) were destined for African territories and this was reflected in the content of the lectures. One man named Coffin was going to a Pacific territory, giving rise to a string of jokes about cannibals, big cooking pots, and deadly diseases. Donald Luddington (later Sir Donald and Governor of the Solomon Islands) and I were due to go to Hong Kong. For me, this choice of destination had occurred in a roundabout way. Having been born in Penang, I had opted for the Malayan Civil Service, but was instead offered Uganda. Finding that Uganda was well inland and far from the coast, I asked the Colonial Office to reconsider. They offered me Hong Kong, I looked it up on the map, thought it sounded all right, and said 'yes'.

At the London School of Economics, Donald and I grew increasingly bored with the continual stream of lectures on Africa. Its colonial history, anthropology, economics, and geography were of little interest to us. We complained and were told that special arrangements would be made for us to learn about the administration of a similar waterfront community. This consisted of attending a meeting of the Stepney Borough Council which turned out to be a splendid slanging match between Councillors, vying with each other in hurling insults and invective. The politest Councillor present, who in correct fashion always addressed the Chairman, was a West Indian.

The other students at the LSE were almost all younger than ourselves, perhaps less mature and certainly more prone to silly ideas. Noticeboards and corridors were plastered with posters on the lines of *Hands off Malaya, Down with Colonialism, Freedom for All*. The men on our colonial course (called the First Devonshire course) felt themselves a cut above this nonsense, believing that our job in our posted territories (as the course lectures emphasised) was to educate local people to their own eventual self-government. Needless to say, we made little contact with the remainder of the LSE, although out of curiosity I did attend a lecture by Harold Laski, a well-known left-winger to the point of communist. To my disappointment, he stuck strictly to the lecture's stated title. He was unlikely to be kept in his job if he did otherwise.

The frustration of the Devonshire men at being back at school when they wanted to get on with the real work in their territory led to increasing bolshiness at the LSE. One lad who had served in the Coldstream Guards always appeared in a blue suit, bowler hat, and

Guards tie. Another was a racing fan who spent his time at lectures reading *Raceform over the Sticks*. Having made his daily selection, he would discreetly slip out, ostensibly to go to the toilet, in reality to the nearest telephone to place his bets. A group of crossword devotees, with heads down, would get on with the puzzle as if making notes, calling perhaps to neighbours 'Have you got 5 across?' 'No, but I can help with 10 down if you're stuck.' Tired of this lack of attention, one long-suffering lecturer actually asked us to get our newspapers turned to the right page before the lecture started, as the rustling was too distracting for him. When a lecturer on colonial history described the establishment of African colonial territories as a disgraceful episode, he was roundly booed, much to his surprise. Thereafter he kept a more discreet tongue. When the time came for an examination at the end of the LSE course, no one had any worries. We were not competing with each other. We simply passed notes round and whispered answers to those who had paid even less attention than ourselves. One young man felt the need to be fortified during the long hours of the examinations, so he armed himself with numerous bottles of ink (only fountain pens in those days; no ball points). But they contained sherry which he was kind enough to share with neighbours.

The one really useful piece of information (for the Africans among us) came from a visiting colonial official who said that, if you find yourself in some distant posting and you tear off a strip of black velvet, for God's sake send her elsewhere when your District Commissioner comes to visit. Otherwise you may be in trouble.

All this sounds as if we were the most useless bunch of larrikins about to be let loose on an unsuspecting colonial public. In reality, it was nothing of the sort. These were serious young men, tired of a year of academic study and anxious to get on with the practical side of their chosen profession. The real learning probably came overseas on the job. It's a sad reflection that few of us on that course actually served our full time in HM Overseas Civil Service. The majority probably became redundant in mid-career as their territory reached independence, forcing them to seek other employment, often in a quite different field.

Were we better administrators after completing the Devonshire course? I doubt it, but ever since I've always enjoyed crossword puzzles. (There was only one more Devonshire course before they closed down, with new appointees thereafter trained in their posted territory.)

Chapter XVII

The District Officer's quarters at 'Dunrose' on the Castle Peak Road consisted of a pre-war bungalow and garden lying a short distance from the road. The house had its own water supply coming from a year-round stream that ran down the steep hillside behind the house and continued to the sea a few hundred yards away. In the cold dry winter when the lawn was under stress, I used to set a sprinkler going overnight to water the lawn (this was not a waste of water, as it would otherwise have ended up in the sea). After one particularly chilly night, there was a circle of frost round the sprinkler which was jammed with droplets of ice hanging from it.

This was unusual. Although in winter the temperature could on occasion drop to 5°C when the more sensitive plants like hibiscus would droop and lose their leaves, freezing point was uncommon. On only one later occasion do I recall frost in HK, and that was up the Peak in the 1970s when the same thing happened with a sprinkler left on the lawn overnight.

Lying between the equator and the Tropic of Cancer, HK is semi-tropical, with summer temperatures up to 35°C (and humidity up to 95 per cent) and winter temperatures down to 5°C. An average 85 inches of rain falls between May and September, with a cool dry winter. November is perhaps the most pleasant month, with a particular luminosity in the sky on some days. This same colouring is noticeable in some of the nineteenth-century paintings in the Museum of Art in HK. Obviously the artists were taken with the condition of the sky, capturing it faithfully.

It so happened that, on a visit to Macao, Margaret and I visited the Protestant cemetery which we found to be neglected, overgrown and in a sad state. It took some searching amongst the bushes to discover the grave of Chinnery, the foremost artist in Canton and Macao of the nineteenth century. In those days, the Chinese Government allowed European traders in Canton to operate from their depots (called factories) only during the winter and without any European women. In summer, the traders shifted to Macao which had no such prohibition against European women. The story goes that Chinnery, an Irishman, travelled to India to escape his wife. When she followed him there, he went to Canton, but she forestalled him by meeting him in Macau.

We complained to Bishop Hall, whom I knew, about the state of the Protestant cemetery in Macao; his see covered HK and South China. He was good enough to take up the matter and arrange for the proper upkeep of the cemetery. He was a remarkable, sturdy man who had been awarded a Military Cross and Bar as an infantry officer in the First World War before later taking up Holy Orders.

In the days before affirmative action emphasised the point, Bishop Hall ordained four women priests in HK: two Chinese and two European. Not to be outdone, women cadets (European and Chinese) were appointed in the Administrative Service, with similar pay and conditions to men; the salary related to the post, not to the holder's sex.

On the opposite side of the Castle Peak Road to 'Dunrose' stood a large two-storey house occupied by an elderly Chinese couple. He was the retired owner of the Blue Taxi fleet which in those days enjoyed almost a monopoly of the taxi business in HK. He liked to potter about his garden looking like one of his gardeners, wearing a singlet, long baggy shorts and thongs. A stranger might tell them apart only by his gold watch and gold-rimmed spectacles. He kindly invited us from time to time to use his swimming pool which had a changing room with an English notice saying 'Do not urinate in the pool'. His wife would always lead us through her Western-style drawing room with furniture and carpets from Harrods in London, still covered in polythene and apparently seldom used. She and her husband preferred a separate Chinese-style room. In a first-floor room, he invited me to look through his powerful telescope which was focussed on Macao some forty or fifty miles away across the mouth of the Pearl river. To keep burglars and kidnappers away, they kept three large and fierce Alsatian dogs in the fenced-off garden overnight. But, like most dogs let loose at night, they spent most of the time barking at nothing and keeping Margaret and I awake. The couple were good enough to arrange things differently when I took the matter up with him. Since he wore a hearing aid that he presumably left off at night, he may not have noticed the barking.

It was in the 1950s that China began to expel European missionaries, many of whom had lived most of their lives in China. The daily train from Canton brought loads of tired, bewildered priests and nuns, with few possessions and little or no idea of what would happen next. Father Poletti, the resident Roman Catholic priest in Tai Po, met the train every day at Lo Wu station on the border where passengers were obliged to disembark on the Chinese side of the bridge, walk across on foot with their baggage, pass through HK immigration and customs before getting on the HK train to Kowloon (neither side allowed its rolling stock across to the other side, for fear of not getting it back again). It was up to each religious denomination to take care of its expelled clergy, the majority being helped back to their country of origin.

Father Poletti was a bearded, voluble Italian who rode a motorcycle with a lighted cigarette burning fiercely between his whiskered lips. In his modest village house in Fanling, he kept a crested mynah in a cage. 'Go on, say Ave Maria, damn you,' he would rage at the bird.

I was approached one day at home by a Chinese who said that he was aware of a load of embargoed goods due to be shipped to China from the Castle Peak coast in the next few days. When I said I would drive him round to the Castle Peak Police Station to report the matter, he was reluctant but eventually agreed. But the European Police Inspector belittled the information and said that the man was unreliable and not to be trusted. I was puzzled by this attitude and failed to understand, as I later came to realise, that the Inspector was probably on the make and being paid to close his eyes. At that stage, in common with much of HK, I was not familiar with the pattern of corruption and certainly not on the lookout for signs of it. In later years, I was all too familiar with it.

Checking the votes in the New Territories at a Rural Committee election in winter (1951).

Driving near Yuen Long one day, I passed the drive leading to the house of Mr Chiu Lut-sau, a community leader whose mother had just died. Hearing the familiar sound of Chinese flute and cymbal, I stopped and entered out of curiosity to have a look at a traditional funeral ceremony. But I found myself grabbed by a master of ceremony who pushed me forward towards the coffin and intoned '*Sarm chee, guk goong*'. Fortunately I knew enough Cantonese to understand that I was required to bow three times towards the coffin and once towards Chiu who was thereafter grateful for my appearance, although unaware that it was accidental. No one had trained me to understand that, in cases of bereavement, the DO ought as a matter of course to pay his respects.

In the winter of 1953, I was asked to officiate at the counting of votes at the election of the new Chairman of a Rural Committee. I was aware that a local dignatory, a brash and pushy individual, was determined to become Chairman and that there was a possibility of irregularity in the voting. Hence the request to me to officiate, in the expectation that I would fail to spot any irregularity and would provide an official seal of respectability to the whole affair. With some misgivings, I accepted.

Sitting at a table counting votes, it became obvious that something fishy was going on. I therefore declined to accept the results and was forced to appear unmoved at the subsequent uproar and furious demands by the would-be Chairman who reminded me that in the 1920s the then DO Tai Po had been assaulted by villagers for an unpopular decision. I sat tight, even when he walked round behind me; I won my point. It was important that everyone should understand the integrity of the District Officer.

Chapter XVIII

Whilst still DO Yuen Long, I became concerned at my lack of knowledge of Chinese custom where it was relevant to my job. It seemed to me that any cadet posted in future as District Officer might be equally handicapped if he was unaware of traditional customs and might thereby unwittingly stir up trouble. For instance, where the owner of agricultural land had applied for its conversion to building status so as to allow him to construct a house, it was too often the case that, on inspection, the house was found to be already under construction without waiting for approval (or disapproval). Asked to explain, the owner would usually say that, since a lucky day was coming up, he could not afford to wait, e.g. for scrutiny of plans, etc. I discovered that this problem could be overcome by instructing the applicant to proceed with ceremonies for house-building without doing any actual building. Details of the ceremonies are shown in Appendix A.

To help myself and future DOs, I compiled the information at Appendix A in the hopes that it would become an official handbook in the District Administration. But there is no evidence that it ever did, and it is unlikely that present residents in the completely changed circumstances of the NT today have the slightest idea of these traditional customs. Once a week or so, I would spend the better part of an afternoon chatting to the Chairman of the Pat Heung Rural Committee, an elderly leader in a long gown, gathering information on customs and cross-checking details. He approved of what I was doing, probably realising better than I that the traditional rural economy and customs of the NT were changing and that a written record was needed before the past was forgotten.

It was a fascinating exercise, undertaken not in the spirit of anthropological research but purely as an aid to the administrative duties of a DO. Having produced the booklet, I was duty-bound to clear it with the District Commissioner, NT, who at that stage was Ken Barnett, formerly the Deputy Colonial Secretary when I first arrived in HK. Ken was a large dark-haired man with a soft voice and tiny handwriting. As a pre-war officer and a member of the HK Defence Force, he had been a POW during the Japanese Occupation when he had perfected his knowledge of Cantonese. Fluent in spoken and written Chinese, he was an acknowledged expert in things Chinese. But he was never a speedy man with his paperwork. My treatise on traditional NT customs disappeared without trace until suddenly one day it reappeared, largely intact.

Ken was married to a Chinese lady. They had no children of their own but, in accordance with custom, had adopted the orphan daughter of Mrs Barnett's sister who had apparently died together with her husband during the War. Ken was a well-known character in HK. On his appointment as DCNT, the Castle Peak Rural Committee invited him to a welcoming dinner in the Castle Peak Hotel. When Ken arrived, he was ushered to a large rattan chair which promptly collapsed, depositing him on the floor. Members of the Rural Committee were horrified at this accident to their honoured guest. Ken was in no way put out, but remarked that he must be getting near his desired weight of two picul. Looking at his bulk, it was hard to disagree. (A picul consists of 100 catties. Since a catty weighs $1^1/3$ pounds, a picul converts to 133 pounds).

The Heung Yee Kuk (an association of elders that covered the whole of the NT) also invited Ken to a welcoming dinner at their offices in Tai Po on the eastern side. Ken was not known for his punctuality but, when half an hour had passed without his appearance, a telephone message to his house in HK indicated that he had departed and must be on his way. Over an hour later, he turned up, full of apologies, to say that en route he realised that he had left his speech behind. (This was long before the first cross-harbour tunnel was built. Vehicles crossed on the vehicular ferry.) When the time came for Ken to make his speech, he produced his notes for it. They consisted of what appeared to be four

Chinese characters on a piece of paper not much larger than a postage stamp. It was doubtless a splendid speech in Chinese, full of classical allusions, but well beyond my standard of fluency.

During this period, on the western side of the NT, the Tai Lam Chung dam and reservoir were under construction. The two or three villages due to be inundated were promised new houses elsewhere and quite happy about the arrangement. Ken thought he had better talk to them in their existing villages which meant a walk of several miles over rough rural paths. So I sent word for villagers to gather at a central village to meet the DCNT. Ken turned up wearing a blue suit and a Homburg hat, apparently feeling that this was appropriate garb for the walk. He was unaffected by the climb through the hills and valleys but disconcerted to find that something had gone wrong and that the gathering of villagers was at a quite different place to where we expected. He would have been justified in being extremely annoyed with me for this confusion but instead was philosophical about the problems of this life.

From time to time, Ken would summon his three DOs for a meeting in his Kowloon office, with an agenda of items to be discussed. It was seldom that we got through the handful of items. On one occasion, not a single item was discussed. Instead, we would be treated to a discourse on the derivation of Chinese place names in the NT; the selection and training of mandarins from the NT under the Ching dynasty; and arrival in earlier centuries of Hakka in the NT from further up the coast. Proceedings at one meeting were disrupted by the entry of a Chinese workman wearing striped pyjamas who used a hammer and chisel to break open a steel filing cabinet. 'Sorry about the noise,' said Ken, 'but my wife lost the keys to the confidential cabinet.'

Pre-war HK (and possibly other Far Eastern territories) seemed to produce characters, bearing in mind that European communities in those days tended to be smaller and life less of a constant rush. This is not to imply that pre-war ability, commercial acumen and general efficiency were in any way lacking. But the more relaxed atmosphere in earlier years appeared to encourage the development of individuals who stood out for one reason or another, not necessarily for sheer proficiency in their particular field but rather for quirks of character that amused or titillated without being nasty or irritating.

The Stanley Military Cemetery contains graves of soldiers and their families dating from the 1840s when Britain first took over HK. There is also a Commonwealth War Graves section with the graves of Servicemen who died in 1941 in the Battle of HK and others who died during subsequent imprisonment by the Japanese. Amongst these prisoners of war are three holders of the George Cross awarded for exploits during imprisonment. A third section in the cemetery contains the graves of civilian internees who died in Stanley internment camp during the War. One of the internees was One-arm Sutton, a well-known character from the period between the two World Wars when he featured large in China, sometimes as bodyguard to a Chinese warlord and at other times as an arms dealer.

At a luncheon with Teddy Lau Chan-kwok at his country residence near Yuen Long, a fellow-guest was a European lawyer who pre-war had successfully defended Ho Chi-min (Uncle Ho of Vietnam) from extradition by the French to Indochina on a charge of subversion. Extradition might have led to imprisonment on Devil's Island off French Guiana. Uncle Ho was so grateful that, after the eventual establishment of Vietnam and his position as leader of the country, he used to invite the lawyer to Vietnam for an annual reunion.

Chapter XIX

The District Office, South, covered the Saikung peninsula, Lantau and other islands. At the start of my time as DO Yuen Long, the DO South was Jimmy Wakefield who had been in the Royal Engineers in HK at the time of the Japanese Occupation. Whilst a POW, he had studied Cantonese with Ken Barnett and post-war was appointed a cadet. Because of his pre-war training as an architect and because the Public Works Department was not then in a position to help, Jimmy was the unofficial NT source for scrutinising and approving building plans up till about 1954 when the PWD took over with professionals. Till then, DOs sent plans to Jimmy who was quick and decisive in commenting. This arrangement may seem absurd in the present-day context, but it worked then because plans were for the most part for simple one- or two-storey structures and there was no other way to do it.

In about 1964, Austin Coates took Jimmy's place as DO South. Son of Eric Coates, the composer, Austin took a lively interest in his parishioners and in Chinese social life. Although his Cantonese was limited, he seemed to have a deeper insight into the ways of ordinary people than most of us. He had already written two excellent books about his wartime contacts with Indian family life, and was in the process of writing another. The first we knew of this was from an incident in the District Office South. The District Commissioner (not Ken Barnett) was apparently walking through the general office when he enquired the identity of an unfamiliar face typing at a government typewriter. The DC, who disliked Austin anyway, was irate to discover that the typist was a private individual engaged by Austin to type the manuscript for Austin's next book. This caused some trouble and Austin did not last long in the job. It turned out to be a splendid book (*Myself a Mandarin*) about the land cases that came Austin's way as Assistant

Refreshments after a function in the New Territories (1951). John Barrow (District Commissioner) is seated (with bow tie) next to Jimmy Wakefield (District Officer, South). I'm standing, with George Roylance (Land Bailiff) behind me.

Land Officer. I last saw Austin in 1994 in Portugal where he lived surrounded by books. He died shortly after from cancer of the throat, possibly brought on by the cigars that he loved to smoke. By no means an ideal civil servant, he lived life to the full, with a happy knack of getting to know people. He was always great friends with numerous Governors of Macao and with leading lights in the Philippines, having produced a life of Rizal, a hero of the Philippine independence movement from Spain at the end of the nineteenth century.

When I first took over as DO Yuen Long, I was approached by a number of villagers dissatisfied by the verdicts handed down by my predecessor sitting as Assistant Land Officer in a land court. On my looking into the cases, I could not understand on what grounds my predecessor had reached his decisions. They appeared contrary to common sense. Furthermore, none of these decisions had been registered as a memorial, as required under the relevant Ordinance; the decisions were accordingly not legally binding. I therefore reopened the cases, checked the evidence again, and sometimes reached different decisions. The word must have spread because thereafter a steady stream of applications began to come in, with the result that I was dealing with at least two hearings a day. Usually I also had a look beforehand at the site in question, in case it showed any important feature not evident from records and evidence. Once, in a dispute over the ownership of an old horseshoe grave, representatives from only one party turned up (the other side must have realised that their claim was spurious). I was peering at the inscription on the headstone when a large lizard leapt out from the undergrowth in front. 'Oh, the representative from the other party is leaving us,' I said. This settled the case.

One of the effects of the embargo on certain goods (useful for military purposes) into or out of China during the Korean War was a shortage of wolfram (or tungsten) for hardening steel. China had hitherto been a main supplier. To overcome the shortage, would-be miners in HK prospected over the hills of the NT, digging trial holes indiscriminately in likely places. The countryside became pockmarked, giving rise in the wet season to erosion and mud in stream courses. The Mines Officer from HK did his best to catch these illegal diggers but made little impact, as it was easy from above to see him coming up a hillside. Furthermore, he was a large and heavy individual, not built for clambering up steep hills. He told me that, at the age of sixteen he had enlisted in the infantry in the First World War when he had been wounded. A pleasant man, he later succumbed like many after him to the greed that HK can foster, and was imprisoned for corruption.

But, before this happened, I accompanied him one day to survey the extent of illegal prospecting and mining round the coast of Castle Peak. With us came the Professor of Geography from the University of HK who lectured us throughout with information about raised beaches, decomposition of granite to form kaolin, and different rock strata. Every now and again the professor would stop and shovel some sand, stone or earth into a bag which he would hand over to his assistant carrying a HK basket made of rattan. By the end of the walk, the unfortunate assistant was bent double under the weight.

Chapter XX

The traditional rural pattern of NT life was slowly changing after the influx of refugees from China following the establishment of the Communist regime in October 1949. Refugees were beginning to farm marginal land, either Crown land or leased private land. In either case, they needed water. Sometimes they dug wells; other times they diverted watercourses. This led to disputes with NT rice farmers who complained that the newcomers were stealing the limited amount of water. Land cases about water rights became commonplace, and visits in each case were essential to assess the merits.

Many of the refugee cultivators were hardworking, transforming barren ground (even sandy beaches) into productive vegetable and fruit growing areas. They could be seen at all hours of the day working the soil, watering with two wooden buckets at either end of a carrying pole, weeding or packing baskets of produce for market. They always seemed to be able to find water by digging, even in the dry season. The produce was fertilised with human nightsoil, diluted in water and causing a dreadful stench. A large proportion of these cultivators were Chiu Chau from further north near Swatow. Argumentative, noisy, and sometimes violent, they tended to clash with the Cantonese of the NT who seldom spoke the Chiu Chau dialect.

One Sunday, I was called upon, with Tommy Cashman (Police Divisional Superintendent, NT), to try and defuse a pending battle between Chiu Chow cultivators and Cantonese landowners irritated at diversion of their traditional water supplies. Each side was drawn up fifty yards apart, armed with farming implements and threatening to use them. Originally placed uncomfortably in the middle to keep the opposing camps apart, we then dashed from one lot to the other until the sun grew so hot that it was possible to persuade them to retire to the shade and discuss face to face with representatives, rather than have two angry taunting mobs inciting each other to violence. Eventually we reached agreement with an uneasy peace. It was then that I began to realise that, no matter how intransigent parties may seem, HK Chinese usually manage to find a solution to a problem. For a time all may seem hopeless, but in the end there is often some sort of consensus.

Tommy Cashman was a big smiling Irishman, brought up pre-war in the quarters of the Lok Ma Chau police station where his father was the officer in charge. (Lok Ma Chau is a rocky hill on the edge of the Shum Chun river near its mouth at Deep Bay in the north of the NT. A narrow road led to it, with a recognised border crossing over the river. Hence the importance of the police station). We met on another occasion at Lau Fau Shan at the edge of Deep Bay where oyster farmers were in dispute. Originally there had been no road out here, but it was not long after the Pacific War that the Government considered the possibility of replacing the increasingly crowded and dangerous Kai Tak airport by a new one on the flat agricultural plain leading to Lau Fau Shan. For this purpose, a tarmac road was constructed for a few miles to allow survey teams to operate. In the end, the Government concluded that the project was not feasible, whereupon the RAF took advantage of the new road to build a few signals and radar installations in the near vicinity. But to get to Lau Fan Shan, it was necessary to walk from the end of the road or to ride a bicycle.

Tommy's next claim to fame occurred at a shootout. In the northern part of the NT, a gunman armed with a pistol hid in a field of sugar cane standing 6 feet high. Tommy's response was not to send someone else in to locate the gunman who, crouching still, would almost certainly hear and see any policeman approaching through the closely packed and rustling stalks of sugar cane. Tommy put on a bullet-proof vest and went in himself. Two of the gunman's bullets hit Tommy on the chest without penetrating before Tommy used his .45 automatic pistol to finish off the gunman. When I asked him about it later, he made light of the whole thing.

Where visits needed to be made for official purposes, it was easy enough to do so by car if the sites were reasonably close to the road. But

Visiting a village by bicycle in winter (1951).

too often, the sites were far from roads. Walking, particularly in the humid heat of summer, was too exhausting and wasted too much time. I therefore made a practice of arranging for villagers to wait at the side of the road with two bicycles: one for me, and one for the interpreter. But it was not all plain sailing. Paths to villages usually led past rice fields, with the path constructed on the bund between two inundated fields and often no more than two feet wide, with a narrow plank over irrigation channels cut through the bund. After wet weather, the paths could be muddy and slippery. There was no room to wobble on the bicycle. On one unfortunate occasion, the interpreter wobbled and fell off into a wet paddy field, to the huge amusement of the local children.

Walking on a narrow path one day, we met a couple of buffalo making their way home behind their owner after ploughing a wet rice field. Buffaloes in the NT take no notice of Chinese villagers but seem to be able to sense outsiders, especially Europeans. Concerned that they might be hostile towards me, I squeezed to one side as much as possible without falling into the wet paddy field. The first buffalo lumbered past without incident and I was beginning to think that the second one would follow suit when it slapped its wet and muddy tail across my stomach. This produced gales of laughter when we reached the village, with predictions that it would lead to the birth of a son. In fact, it led to a daughter.

In the 1950s, the military garrison of Divisional strength needed training and firing areas to prepare against possible Chinese invasion. The Castle Peak, a lofty mountain, was officially made an artillery range for 25-pounders, with a couple of villagers paid by the Army to hoist red flags on firing days. It was my business to warn local residents not to venture near there when the red flag was hoisted. It was the Army's business to make sure that the area was clear of people before firing. This was far from easy, as scrap metal scavengers, oblivious to the danger of blinds, hunted for fragments on non-firing days and were often too close during firing. The same applied to the Army's small arms range at Lo Wu.

There were several firing points for the Castle Peak artillery range, mostly close to the main road. More than once, driving along I failed to notice a troop of guns hidden behind a hill and nearly swerved off the road when they all fired simultaneously. These military activities were all part of the prevailing worry that China might decide to invade HK. Whether HK could in fact defend itself was another matter, but at least HK must be seen to be prepared to do so, particularly to keep up local morale. Despite a small group of noisy left-wingers, the majority of HK residents were anti-communist and had left China for that reason. It was important for the HK Government to act in a manner to secure their continued support.

Chapter XXI

The pattern of administration in the pre-computer days was probably quite different to what it is now. All paperwork and discussion were in English. Every topic and subject had its own file which circulated round the department by means of minutes addressed up or down the line. It was normally improper to send a file to another department, since it might get stuck there or even disappear. A minute from a junior officer might seek approval from a more senior officer for a particular course of action. Minutes could be handwritten but, since more senior officers usually had their own secretary or access to one and since some handwriting could be poor, minutes latterly tended to be typed. I always insisted on all mine being typed, on the principle that a typed message had greater impact than a possibly illegible handwritten one, however compelling its content.

Where it was necessary to consult another department or to reply to a memorandum (always shortened to memo) from one, a typed memo would be sent and signed pro head of department. The convention was that memos between departments were communications between the respective heads of department. It was wrong to address a memo to any officer within the department. A memo signed by the head of a department required a reply signed by the head of the department addressed and not by a more junior officer. Memos always carried the reference number of the files from which they emanated, so that the reply could be readily entered into the correct file.

If a minute had been placed in a file, the designation of the officer to whom the minute was addressed was written in the distribution ladder on the file cover, so that the messenger who periodically emptied the Out tray during the day could carry the file direct to its addressee. Every day a clerk from the file registry was required to record all files in each officer's In and Out trays, so that there was some record of where files were. Lost and strayed files were the bane of the registry's life.

In the days before photocopiers, it was necessary for a typist to type the text on to a waxed sheet of paper which the officer concerned would sign with a stylus before the sheet was placed in a Gestetner machine. This was effective, producing a number of copies, but it was cumbersome and the waxed sheet was difficult to check, consisting not of black type but of scratches in white wax.

Chinese office staff were required to possess an adequate command of spoken and written English for their particular duties. This requirement diminished further down the line. Menial staff such as drivers, sweepers and gardeners might acquire some English but it was not normally expected of them. All letters to Chinese were sent with Chinese and English versions. I always signed my Chinese letters with my Chinese name. On first appointment in HK, all cadet officers were supplied by the SCA with an official Chinese name which sounded vaguely like their English name and followed the Chinese tradition of linking virtue with nature. My anglicised name was Wai Lau-san which translates into Present Willow Tree New. It was customary to arrange for the printing of a business card (complete with honorifics and official designation) with English on one side and Chinese on the other. This card was handed out on introduction to strangers. The official languages in HK were English and Chinese, and this was reflected in street names and public notices. Latterly there was some disquiet about placing an English version above the Chinese one. Where there was enough space for the purpose, it was policy to place the two versions side by side rather than one above the other.

Confidential files were kept and handled in a Confidential Registry by special staff. Confidential memos were placed in envelopes sealed with sealing wax and embossed with a coat of arms. Senior officers in sensitive posts had secretaries with higher security clearance, usually Europeans. In the 1950s, it was difficult to recruit Chinese secretaries with the requisite standard of English and of skills in typing and shorthand. So there was much reliance on recruiting suitable Europeans, bearing in mind that the Government was competing with the bigger Western companies such as Jardines and the HK Bank, often prepared to offer a higher salary. The recruitment of government secretaries was in the hands of the Chief Clerk, an active and forceful man called Dick Maynard, who liked files to be kept tidy and was not above drawing the attention of senior officers to their sloppy efforts. An apocryphal story relates that Dick was approached one day by a suitable European lady seeking to become a secretary. Dick promptly engaged her on day-to-day terms pending the results of her medical examination and permanent appointment. Part of this process required the lady to provide a urine specimen. She promised to do so but, when time had elapsed without a specimen, Dick reminded her. Still no specimen. Fearful of losing a suitable secretary and too embarrassed to remind the lady again, Dick did the obvious and produced a specimen himself which he sent to the Medical Department. In due course, back came the reply from the Medical Department, to say that this candidate should not be engaged as she was pregnant. Dick therefore applied for maternity leave.

Chapter XXII

Posted to the Secretariat, I became an Assistant Secretary responsible for the day-to-day business of government activities in the middle range of the alphabet: labour, marine, mining, narcotics, post and telegraph. With not much experience of the Government, I had never visited most of these departments and knew little or nothing about their duties. It seems incredible these days to realise the ignorance of a civil servant expected to handle matters about which he was largely in the dark. But life was a struggle in those days to try to catch up. Induction courses came later.

Realising my limitations, I suggested to the Deputy Colonial Secretary (to whom I was responsible) that I should visit the Marine Department and be shown the range of their activities. The DCS had recently transferred from another territory. Agreeing to my proposal, he decided to come as well. This dismayed me as it meant an official visit by him and not a low-level fact-finding approach with me asking the questions. We set off in his official car westwards through the city which was bedecked in Nationalist flags, it being 10 October, the Double Tenth, the official Nationalist day when Sun Yat-sen declared the first Chinese republic in 1911. The DCS peered out and asked what all the flags were for. Astonished at his ignorance, I explained, pointing out that the two days in the year when there might be unrest were 1 October (Chinese Communist day) and 10 October (Chinese Nationalist day). Each side was liable to taunt the other and provoke trouble. The visit to the Marine Department was not a success.

The next visit (to the Commerce and Industry Department) overloaded me with so much information that I could hardly remember anything. A clear picture remains of a large vault full of confiscated gold bars. Gold was a controlled commodity, the object being to prevent national economies from being drained of resources. We were told that, if we could pick up a gold bar, we were welcome to take it away. Needless to say, each bar was too heavy to lift unaided. Nonetheless, I did at least understand that most of the department's work lay in promoting the worldwide sale of HK goods. From its pre-war and immediately post-war status as an entrepot port, bringing in overseas goods for distribution into China and South-East Asia, HK was now turning into a manufacturing centre. This had begun in 1949-50 with the cotton mills set up in HK by Shanghai industrialists fleeing from the Communists. They were reputed to have brought down the actual machinery and workers. From this beginning, others had branched out into all sorts of light industry: vacuum flasks, torches, rubber boots, etc. There was more than enough labour in HK for these burgeoning industries, many of which started up in a small way on hillsides or vacant ground, without official permission or security of tenure. Official histories describe this aspect and the unfortunate fires that swept squatter colonies, leading to the Government's decision to introduce a resettlement programme for people and for industry.

Happily the period in the Secretariat did not last long. My next move was to the Defence Branch which was entirely staffed by Europeans. Most of the Branch's work consisted of preparing or reviewing contingency plans in the event of an emergency. This covered internal unrest and external threat, apart from policy relating to the HK Royal Naval Reserve, the HK Regiment (volunteers), and the Royal Hong Kong Auxiliary Air Force, the Essential Services Corps, the Civil Aid Service, and the Auxiliary Medical Service. It was a reassuring feature that so many Chinese volunteered for the various services and found themselves doing useful work. For instance, the Civil Aid Service and Auxiliary Medical Service (trained, amongst other things, in rescue work) were frequently called out after big fires, typhoons, floods and similar disasters, to assist in rescuing victims from house collapse etc. The ESC was likely to be called upon in the event of internal or external threat, and at one stage even required its members to take part in training in pistol shooting. This was the last occasion after the Second World War that I ever fired a pistol.

Entry into the Defence Branch was through a large reinforced steel door with two combination locks. Inside that was a grille door with a key lock. My office was locked with a key whenever I left it. In my office was a safe with a combination lock. Only the Defence Secretary and myself (the Assistant) knew the combinations for the big outer door. This meant that I had to be early to the office every morning to allow staff entry (and was last to leave in the evening). If I was late in the morning, I had to run the gauntlet of a group full of unhelpful suggestions as I attempted to concentrate on remembering two lots of combination numbers. With my own safe, this made three sets of numbers that I had to memorise. To make matters worse, all these combinations had to be changed (by me) once a quarter. It was noticeable how much easier it was to memorise if I locked and unlocked every day. Frequent practice seemed to oil the mental wheels.

At this point, work had progressed on demolishing the old Secretariat building in stages and simultaneously erecting the new one on more or less the same site. One of the first offices to move was the Defence Branch which was provided with larger premises and an underground Emergency Control Centre. We shifted everything across to the new offices with high security measures to ensure no breach in transit. To comply with floor loading, the massive safes were sited over reinforcing beams and everyone looked forward to even more hush-hush activities.

Chapter XXIII

Returning in 1958 from my second four-year tour in HK, I was posted as an Assistant Director of Urban Services responsible for city cleansing. This covered the collection of refuse and nightsoil, public toilets, public bath houses, disposal of the dead, and the management of public bathing beaches (although nothing to do with cleansing, it was convenient to lump them in with cleansing). My office was on the top floor of the former General Post Office building, since demolished; the site is now occupied by World Wide House. The old building dated from the last part of the nineteenth century, with turrets and external frippery in what appeared to be an Imperial Indian style of architecture. The Post Office on the ground floor was entered up steps, giving way to a huge hall and ceiling fans. High up on the wall opposite the entrance was a notice (in English) reading 'As water to the thirsting soul is a letter from a far place'.

Access to the top floor was either up a splendid, lengthy staircase of teak or in a lift that must have been installed at the same time as the building was constructed. It held only two or three people and consisted of expanding iron all round; you might lose it if you so much as poked a finger out through the gaps. Needless to say, the lift took ages to go up or down.

To increase space, the open-air verandah round the top floor had been enclosed to form part of the offices, despite the green tiling on its floor and the surface gutters next to the outer wall and discharging at the corners. In fact, the gutters were useful as the roof leaked like a sieve. When it rained, the water poured through in various places. Buckets and basins would be sited under leaks, together with hessian sacks in slippery corners. The toilets were the wettest spots. A visit there always meant taking an umbrella with you if you did not wish to be soaked.

I was fascinated with the new job. It really brought you into contact with how the local population lived, their everyday problems, and the patience with which they put up with discomfort and inconvenience. The Urban Services Dept was responsible inter alia for collecting domestic and street refuse from HK and Kowloon (not the NT in those days; in fact, there was no collection at all in the NT which was largely rural). This responsibility was discharged by an army of street sweepers, each allocated a beat of several streets which had to be swept on both sides, including the pavements. Only public areas were swept, not private land. Each beat sweeper was armed with a brush, a shovel and a hand cart containing two bins. Swept-up refuse was placed in the bins which were emptied in due course into containers at a refuse collecting point. Throughout the day, a vehicle would collect the refuse and discharge it at designated waterfront wharves into a barge. A couple of barges either side of a tug would then make their way to the refuse dump at Gin Drinkers Bay on the south-west side of the NT where gangs of labourers would empty the barges by hand into baskets, carrying them to the edge of the reclamation. A bulldozer travelled up and down compacting newly formed sections of reclamation before lorries brought in soil to cover every day's load of refuse as a means of keeping down fly-breeding, rats, and smell. The public was excluded from the refuse dump because it would have let in scavengers digging holes and causing a nuisance.

The whole process from street-sweeping to refuse dump was recognised as labour-intensive and cumbersome, but it worked. The main object was to ensure that refuse was not left unattended in the hot humid summer weather of HK, breeding flies and rats. Every effort was made to streamline the process, from improving the type of brush (which used to wear out too quickly) to replacing bamboo baskets on handcarts by plastic containers. Brightly coloured litter baskets that did not fill up with water when it rained were sited strategically round the city to reduce the incidence of litter discarded on the ground. Periodically the refuse dump at Gin Drinkers Bay was sprayed to keep down flybreeding. Whenever I visited, it was necessary to tuck the ends of my trousers into my socks to stop cockroaches running up my legs.

Since the USD collected refuse only from public places, householders were required to bring their domestic refuse to a refuse collecting point. For many upper-storey residents, this was a nuisance, to be overcome by employing a private refuse collector, usually a woman, who (in return for a modest fee) collected daily from the household and dumped the refuse at the collecting point. She probably did a bit of salvaging too.

The older parts of HK and Kowloon still contained pre-war tenement houses that had no flush toilets. Householders used whatever container took their fancy and placed it for disposal on the landing outside their front door. Every day after midnight, a gang of USD women collected the container, carried it to a specialised vehicle where it was emptied, washed and sterilised before its return to the landing. It was a dirty, unpleasant job, but there was never any lack of labour in the period up till all these tenement buildings were replaced by flats with flush toilets. When visiting, I was always filled with admiration at the way these women made their way up and down dark staircases carrying spillable loads. We arranged the use of torches tied to the women's foreheads but they were not always popular. This emphasised the point that it is unwise to go ahead with so-called improvements until they have first been tried out by staff, who are sometimes traditional in outlook and reluctant at first to accept new ways of doing things. Rushing ahead with practical remedies can be counter-productive unless prejudice is first overcome. A prime example of this occurred when a beat sweeper about his work on a road was killed by a vehicle. A proposal to issue beat sweepers with bright orange or green waistcoats met strong opposition. I was told: 'We wouldn't consider doing this strenuous dirty job if we weren't desperate for work. It's adding insult to injury to make us wear a garment that singles us out in the public eye. We don't want to come to public notice. As for the danger from traffic, we'd rather take our chances without this jacket.' I therefore backed off and bided my time. Sooner or later, the tide would turn. The trick was to recognise the moment when it came.

Public toilets used to be terrible. You could smell them from yards away. But they were important. They were needed not just for the passing trade. During the day, a sizeable part of the public lived on the street: labourers, rickshaw pullers, hawkers, shopkeepers, etc. These people required toilets and proper disposal of the contents to avoid health problems and nuisance. When I first started the job, the urinals in male toilets were often blocked by cigarette butts and litter, with the result that the flushing was useless. The remainder of the toilets consisted of an open channel over which men were expected to squat, with a half door in front to offer some privacy. No toilet paper was provided. At regular intervals, the channel was flushed by a surge of water, often to the dismay of those squatting. Since newspaper and other forms of insoluble paper were used as toilet paper, more blockages were liable to occur. Over the years, it was possible to provide individual urinals, with mothballs at the outlets to keep down smell; individual cubicles with lockable doors and free toilet paper; an equal number of cubicles in the ladies' toilets as in the men's (previously ladies' toilets contained fewer cubicles than the adjoining men's, although demographically the sexes are roughly equal in numbers and ladies tend to take longer). Public toilets in HK are now clean, bright, efficient in operation, and discreetly sited in the areas of greatest need.

Public bath houses seem peculiar to HK, but again they were a health requirement to meet the lack of washing facilities in tenement buildings that in any case were often crowded and short of privacy. Even when tenement buildings were demolished, the demand for bath houses continued. Usually attached to public toilets, they offered individual cubicles with showers and hot and cold water. Both bath houses and public toilets were free of charge. But a small charge was made for removal of nightsoil. Since this charge could be a deterrent, leading to dumping of nightsoil in public places, I sent a memo to the Financial Secretary seeking approval in principle for deleting the charge, pointing out that any health risk from dumping would not be confined to the household concerned but to the public at large. The total sum to be foregone was negligible. In other words, the proposal made sense. The FS was an Irishman nearing the end of his service and probably getting a bit big for his boots. He turned the proposal down without explanation. Happily his successor took a more sensible view.

The FS must have upset the Governor somehow, because he never received the expected knighthood before retirement.

Disposal of the dead is a subject more likely to arouse distate and a shudder than a flicker of real interest. In fact, I found it absorbing because of the traditions, beliefs and customs surrounding it. After many visits to funeral parlours, undertakers and cemeteries, I provided an article on the subject for the HK Branch of the Royal Asiatic Society; see Appendix B. This must have been written some time between 1958 and 1961. These days, the vast majority of HK dead are cremated, largely because the fees are kept below those for burial. There is little point in allowing the dead to occupy more and more burial space in a crowded place like HK, to the exclusion of the living. Cremated ashes pose no health risk and can be kept at home, or in a Buddhist monastery, or in a government columbarium.

Few wish to be associated with disposal of the dead and all expect arrangements to work like clockwork if a bereavement occurs. From the official point of view, this meant keeping an eye on the annual death rate, with a forward projection of five years to ensure that the number of cremators and columbarium spaces would meet the expected demand. Sufficient lead time had to be left for any construction work needed to make up a projected shortfall.

I was approached one day by leaders of the charitable Tung Wah Group of Hospitals to ask whether I would officiate at the opening of their Farewell Pavilion at Diamond Hill in Kowloon. This building would provide a free or subsidised funeral parlour for the poor. It was only too obvious that, with the well-known Chinese aversion to being closely associated with the dead, no Director of the Tung Wah was willing to do the honours and have his name inscribed on a plaque there. I was happy to assist.

The bustle round cemeteries at the two annual grave-worshipping festivals of Ching Ming and Chung Yeung had to be seen to be believed. These were seldom days of mourning, rather of following tradition coupled with a picnic. Exhumed remains would be cleaned with newspaper or anything handy; incense burnt; joss sticks lit, with much genuflection, before being placed at the grave; offerings put in place. At the Tung Wah cemetery in Sandy Bay, I once saw a family enjoying a picnic at the grave which had a Christian cross with a transistor radio hanging from the cross giving forth most unChristian music. The approaches to another cemetery were lined with opportunist beggars seeking alms from the devout. One of the beggars had bloodstained bandages over his legs and arms, presenting a pitiable sight. On seeing me, he gave a radiant smile and greeted me warmly. He normally hawked vegetables and fruit round houses up the Peak, and was as sound in limb as myself. On my departure, he resumed his weeping and wailing.

The management of public bathing beaches grew more complex as time passed. Pre-war, few Chinese bathed in the sea, partly because they did not know how to swim and partly because they disliked becoming sunburnt and looking like peasants or coolies. Post-war, this attitude changed. More and more Chinese, particularly young people, took to the water and expected to enjoy themselves. There were twelve public bathing beaches (all sandy) on HK island; none in Kowloon. Bathing was largely confined to the summer, the weather and the sea being too cold at other times. The most popular beach was at Repulse Bay which at weekends in summer could be so crowded as to cover the sand completely.

Apart from the obvious task of keeping the beach clean, both by hand and by machine, the next need was to define the swimming area by means of connected floats so as to exclude pleasure craft. It astonishes me to see beaches elsewhere with pleasure craft in amongst the swimmers. This is surely tempting accidents. Every HK beach had a complement of official lifesavers trained in rescue and resuscitation. It was up to the lookout on a tower to watch for swimmers in difficulties. Too often, parents failed to supervise children adequately or weak swimmers got out of their depth. The lookout would blow a whistle and point to the swimmer concerned, as patrolling lifeguards rushed to the rescue.

In addition to bathing beaches, there were public swimming pools, usually built on a standard pattern of a main 50-metre pool, a separate diving pool, a shallow training pool, and a toddlers' paddling pool.

Classes to teach people how to swim were held in the training pool. There was a small charge for entry to the swimming pool and, at popular times, a time limit to ensure a turnover of swimmers. In the course of time, improvements included recreational pools with artificial waves, water chutes, and similar devices to entertain those not wishing to swim up and down.

Chapter XXIV

The Urban Services Department was in the unusual position for a government department of working to the orders of the Urban Council (in respect of the urban areas) and not of the Colonial Secretary, but to the orders of the CS in respect of the NT where the jurisdiction of the UC did not run. Although the departmental staff were all civil servants and their salaries were paid by the Government, it was the Urban Council that decided policy and allocated funds for urban projects. In those days, some of the Councillors were appointed by the Government (including a few heads of departments who were ex officio members) and the remainder were elected by ratepayers. The Council elected its own chairman from amongst its members and had its own source of funds consisting mostly of a share of the rates raised by the Government but also including fees and charges for various licences. Work was conducted by means of Select Committees on various aspects such as cleansing, recreation and amenities, public libraries, museums, abattoirs. Although the elected members were divided between two political parties, they seemed to spend more time attacking the Government than each other. But, by and large most Councillors gave good service, learning their subjects and taking the interests of HK to heart rather than indulging in idle point-scoring. The elected members seldom gave the government staff credit for knowing their jobs, but carried on a ceaseless campaign of criticism.

For a number of years, chairmanship of the Urban Council rested with A. de O. Sales (pronounced Sarlez), a long-time resident of HK and local businessman. With a firm grasp of finances, sound common sense, and great integrity, he guided the Council on honest and practical lines in the interests of the people of HK. As an appointed (not elected) member, he was not concerned with party politics and could concentrate on the public good.

Those were the days when civil servants expected to function behind the scenes without coming into the public eye and certainly without interviews by the publicity media. Consequently, too many civil servants, in particular senior ones, were tongue-tied and made to look incompetent when on their hind legs and interviewed by persistent reporters. Monthly Urban Council meetings open to the public were sometimes an embarrassment when civil servants, frozen-faced and uncomfortable, were confronted with probing questions that ignored deference to rank and position. Realising that its public image was slipping, the Government in due course held a series of workshops organised by Radio HK and the Public Information Service. Jimmy Hawthorn, the Director of Radio HK and a north of Ireland man, took us through the full range of radio interviews, reading scripts, discussion groups, and the best way to stand up for yourself. 'That was a beautiful interview you gave, Brian. Your wooden voice came over superbly. Now let's do it again how it should be done.'

In the 1950s and 1960s, the elected Urban Councillors were the sole elected leaders in the administration of HK. Mr Chris Patten, the last Governor before HK was handed back to China on 30 June 1997, emphasised the lack of democracy and the need for a fully elected legislature. This line followed the Western principle that every country ought to be governed by a Westminster style of elected democratic government. But of all Britain's former colonial territories that have become independent since the Second World War, hardly a one now follows the proper democratic system. Some point to Singapore as a shining example, but critics say it is more a guided democracy. There is a fair case for arguing that Westminster democracy may not be suited to all countries, some of which prefer tribal supremacy or some other arrangement. No one seems to have produced a formula to match the requirements of each newly independent country rather than force them all into the straitjacket of Westminster democracy. The straitjacket needed tailoring, but sadly this was overlooked, probably not even realised.

The electorate for the Urban Council was small. Even so, at the regular elections, never more than 20 per cent of the electorate ever bothered to vote. There was clearly no evidence of frustrated electors denied the chance to vote. At every election, I would lead a group of departmental staff, all of them electors, to the polling booth suggesting which of the candidates they should vote for. As I attended all Select Committee meetings, I was in a strong position to know the calibre of candidates. I always chose one who seldom opened his mouth at meetings and tended to decide in favour of the course recommended by the department. This ensured a peaceful run.

By the 1970s, the Government had introduced a system of advisory committees, covering roughly every aspect of administration (except for the responsibilities of the Urban Council). Under an unofficial chairman, the few officials on each committee were obliged to follow the chairman's decision, but if they violently disagreed they could appeal to the Governor. Although the unofficial chairman was appointed by the Government and not elected, he nonetheless represented the interests of that particular field and was generally a leader in it. A drawback to Westminster democracy is that almost every elected member belongs to a party and is obliged to vote on party lines. There is not much scope for individual discretion. The appointed unofficial chairman on the advisory committee could on the other hand take an objective view, usually after consulting his colleagues in that particular field, and by no means always accepted the Government's view.

There was a general feeling in HK that it was preferable to have an older, wealthy leader helping the Government rather than a younger, poorer man who might be on the make. It was a noticeable feature in HK how the really wealthy not only donated money to charity and to public foundations but also came forward to take part free of charge on the committees of voluntary organisations and various government bodies. Critics might claim that this altruism was a matter of seeking personal publicity. Be that as it may, there is no denying the immense amount of help that leading Chinese gave to the community and to building up in HK what amounted almost to a national identity.

It was in the 1970s that the Governor, Sir Murray MacLehose, introduced a system of District Boards as a form of local democracy. The urban areas, and later the NT, were divided into areas, each under a District Board of partly appointed and partly elected members whose duty it was to represent local interests. At first, the District Boards had no real executive authority but could only advise the Government or the Urban Council, and they had only a small source of funds. But, as the Boards grew in popularity and experience, they gradually acquired more executive powers and were the predecessors of the present democratic system of government in HK. Up till then, the HK Government had exercised the usual paternal method of direct colonial government, trying as far as possible to consult local feelings whilst reserving power to itself. This worked adequately but, with increasing education, sophistication, and knowledge of the Western world, the time had come for HK people to manage their own affairs. There was enough material amongst its leading citizens to provide the necessary directorate. Furthermore, with a government policy of localisation, the civil service from top to bottom was more than half filled with Chinese capable of running the affairs of HK.

Chapter XXV

As the years passed, it became apparent that more effective steps were needed to control the mass of hawkers taking over ever more stretches of roads and pavements. Legally no one was allowed to hawk without a licence, and these were broken down into itinerant hawkers licence, fixed pitch, cooked food stall, and so on. But, in practice, thousands hawked without a licence, setting up permanent stalls in certain streets, with electric wiring connected illegally to nearby premises. The original view had been that fixed-pitch licences should be issued only to disabled applicants unable to find other work but they soon proved to be no match for unscrupulous able-bodied who pushed them out of the way. From the point of view of a hawker, if he sited himself where he obstructed pedestrian traffic, he was halfway to making a sale. The fact that pedestrians had difficulty threading their way through the congestion and avoiding the accumulated refuse underfoot never bothered the hawker in his pursuit of making a living. Although licensed hawkers and adjoining shopkeepers might complain of unfair competition from unlicensed hawkers, it was nonetheless the case that public sympathy tended to lie with hawkers and not with official control which was seen as a callous attempt to break the hawkers' rice bowl, leaving them with no other means of subsistence. It was clear that merely taking unlicensed hawkers to Court and arranging for the confiscation of their goods were not the answer, especially as Magistrates indicated their reluctance to convict in support of what they regarded as purely negative and repressive measures.

A policy was therefore adopted of providing new multi-storey markets to replace older inadequate ones, with the inclusion of space inside for enough hawker stalls to house all the on-street hawkers from a particular area. The hawkers concerned welcomed the idea because it sited them where there would be plenty of business, under cover, with water, electricity, storage space, regular cleaning, and security of tenure. Finding the money, suitable sites, and fitting the projects into the capital works programme was a slow and ongoing process. But it moved along and proved a great success, provided adequate control was exercised to ensure that a new lot of hawkers did not occupy the vacated on-road spaces. Initial clearances produced amazing results. It began with the on-road hawkers moving into their allotted stalls in the multi-storey market (up and down escalators), leaving their on-road stalls behind. Staff of the Urban Services Department then demolished and removed the stalls and rubbish, washed down the area, and revealed streets and pavements that had not seen the light of day for possibly years. As an unfortunate side issue, nearby householders then reported an increase in the number of rats, no doubt as a result of the removal of the stalls and source of food.

It was an interesting feature to consider why hawkers existed, and why hawking was so popular amongst those with no particular skills in other directions. The answer lay in the fact that many members of the public preferred to shop at hawker stalls because they were conveniently sited and made it easy to compare prices and quality. On the other hand, it could be argued that shops and market stallholders offered the same. Furthermore, hawkers did not necessarily charge less than shopkeepers. There was as much in favour of one as of the other. But nonetheless a hawker stall in a favourable location usually did good business, aided by the Cantonese preference for daily shopping to ensure fresh produce.

Chapter XXVl

In 1961 I fell foul of an Urban Councillor who attempted to order me to arrange for the installation of a water tap at a cooked food bazaar. On reflection, I realise that I was in the wrong and that the need for the tap was reasonable. But, at the time, I was adamant that I did not take orders from individual Councillors but only from a Select Committee or the Director of Urban Services, neither of whom had made any such request. When the Councillor complained to the Director, I was posted elsewhere in forty-eight hours. I had no respect for the Director anyway. The Councillor and I later got on well together.

My new posting was as Chief Assistant to the Secretary for Chinese Affairs. So it was back to the Fire Brigade Building on the waterfront of HK. I was bemused at first to find that the main topic at the daily departmental meeting was to agree on who would attend the various social functions that evening. Apparently it was important in the interests of departmental relations to attend these functions and to show friendliness with those in charge of leading Chinese charitable organisations like the Tung Wah group of hospitals and the Po Leung Kuk (home for girls). I gradually came to realise that the department operated with a different outlook to other government departments. In traditional Chinese fashion, personal relationships were essential. You did business with someone else only if you had been introduced to him and therefore had some assurance of his bona fides. The Western way of impersonally looking someone up in a trade directory or the telephone book was not acceptable. For the SCA to keep abreast of local Chinese views and aspirations, he had to know the trend-setters personally and keep his ear to the ground. It was his duty to warn the Government of impending problems and of prevailing Chinese opinion. There was an ever-present threat of communist subversion, against which every effort

116

should be made to ensure that the local population was happy with the current regime.

In this connection, it was noticeable that Cantonese opera was faring badly against increasing competition from mainland companies visiting HK and producing Peking opera in Mandarin. Much of the trouble lay in the fact that there were few venues for Chinese opera in HK and certainly no dedicated theatre with a training school, workshops for costumes and scenery, and an administrative centre. The Central Theatre dating from pre-war showed Chinese opera but was inadequate as a training base. It was a typical easy-going venue from a less demanding age. It smelt of drains; hawkers selling wooden swords and cups of tea plied the aisles during performances and theatre-goers came and went through the lengthy operas. On one occasion, a backdrop slipped from an overhead hoist and hid the hero who was then obliged to jump about to show himself.

I tried to interest Sir Tang Shiu-kin into financing a proper theatre for the purpose. A wealthy man, he was known to be keen on Chinese opera but he did not see this as a worthwhile business venture. So Cantonese opera stayed in the doldrums, whilst mainland opera like *Taking Table Mountain by Storm* continued to flourish. Few Europeans could stand the screeching falsettos of Chinese opera, but it was always popular with Chinese audiences. Some of the problem was relieved in later years when the Urban Council adopted a policy of providing theatres in different districts as venues for Chinese opera, school performances, pop groups, and any other suitable activity.

Checking on outstanding paperwork in the department, I was dismayed to find that nothing had been done about a couple of cases where injury had been caused and no compensation paid. Huge quantities of stone were required in HK for concreting and construction work. With so much rock in the territory, there was little problem in providing the rock and crushing it for aggregate. But quarries that had once been sited away from built-up areas often found themselves uncomfortably close as housing spread further afield. In this case, a quarrying contractor had used too much explosive, sending a rock flying into an apartment block where it injured a young girl. I visited the family, found that the girl's injuries had been treated free of charge by the Medical Department, but no compensation had been paid by the contractor. This was duly arranged administratively, although it might have been taken into account when the contractor was prosecuted.

In the other case, the Police raided a group of unlicensed food hawkers; this was common practice to avoid disease from unhygienic cooking and poor cleaning. As the hawking paraphernalia was being put into the back of a lorry as a court exhibit, heated oil from a stove splashed on to a young girl nearby, burning her severely. She had been treated in hospital but still carried disfiguring keloid scars on her face and body. I arranged for the Medical Department to deal with the scars and wanted to speak to the father who worked with the Tramway Company on HK island. After securing the agreement of the general manager to my speaking to a member of his staff, I interviewed the father in the only convenient place: the interior of a tram under repair in the workshop.

The purpose of mentioning these two cases is to indicate part of the job of the SCA, and that was to show that the Government was a caring one anxious to assist its citizens fairly. Without the hearts and minds of the population behind the Government and a growing sense of HK's own identity, administration might otherwise be an uphill task.

One of the subjects coming under the SCA at that time was narcotics, but there seemed to be no departmental action on producing policy. When I took this up, I discovered that the Police and the Customs Service which were the two bodies most involved on the ground were mutually suspicious of each other and consequently did not share intelligence. This did not seem appropriate. Meetings that I arranged between the two bodies made some progress in thawing the ice and in agreeing on overall tactics. It was a small start in combatting what has become a worldwide scourge. The profits to be made from trafficking in narcotics can be so huge that the operators can afford to pay enormous bribes to those responsible for law-enforcement. One of the sadder aspects of narcotics is the extent to which otherwise reasonable law-enforcers can sometimes be seduced into corruption by the chance to acquire undreamed-of riches.

In my earlier days in the Urban Services Department, I had frequent occasion to go to one of their depots in Kennedy Town. This was a pre-war building or rather a series of roofed structures with open sides, housing a number of large woks (fixed, saucer-shaped, iron cooking pots) and a fire box beneath. Before the Second World War, the HK Government in company with the Crown colony of the Straits Settlements (Penang, Singapore and a few other places) operated an official scheme for providing opium for registered opium addicts, in an attempt to cut the ground from under the feet of illegal traffickers. The Kennedy Town premises were the site for cooking and preparing the opium. The premises have long since been demolished and the site used for other purposes.

The Secretary for Chinese Affairs mentioned to me one day that a leading Chinese philanthropist was reported to be very ill, which was unfortunate as the SCA held a cheque for a million dollars from him, intended for a foundation not yet created. Apparently the SCA had kept the cheque in his safe for some time, waiting for some formality to be completed. Astonished that the cheque had not at once been placed in a deposit account to draw interest, I suggested that immediate action be taken to complete the formality before the philanthropist died. To forestall any further delay, I undertook this job myself (the philanthropist died a couple of days later). In later years, the Government's financial regulations were even more explicit in requiring any money received to be banked at once. These days civil servants in HK might be horrified at this instance which is an example of how the Government had to learn from experience. It would be wrong to assume that current requirement and practice were equally applicable years ago when conditions were different and weaknesses perhaps not so pronounced.

One of my other duties in the SCA was to sit as one of the three members of a Film Censorship Board of Review. In those days, all films for public exhibition were required to be passed by a censor whose duty it was to refuse, or require cuts to, films that were too full of sex, blasphemous towards a religion (Buddhist, Taoist, Moslem, Christian), subversive, or otherwise unsuitable. Where a film had been turned down, the distributor had a right of appeal to the Board of Review. In this case, the Chinese distributor (a State agency of the Chinese Government) had appealed, so the Board duly watched the film at our usual hour of 9 a.m. on a Monday morning. The film was a medical one that showed an unfortunate Chinese man sitting on a wooden bench in a corridor (presumably in a hospital) with the severed part of his arm lying on the bench beside him. The story continued with close-ups of the operation to sew the arm back on to the stump. From first to last, the film was enough to make one feel ill, and was certainly not something fit for general exhibition. The distributor continued to agitate and could not understand our insistence that his film was neither entertainment nor in the public interest.

Chapter XXVII

As part of its campaign against narcotics, the Government in the 1960s sponsored a scheme for the rehabilitation of drug addicts. The Society for the Aid and Rehabilitation of Drug Addicts (SARDA) operated under legislation whereby a drug addict could voluntarily undergo a course of treatment for six months, during which time he was forced to remain at the treatment centre. In other words, once committed, he surrendered his freedom for six months and could not cut it short. At the end of that time, a welfare officer of SARDA helped the cured addict to find employment, away from his former environment where pushers and traffickers were likely to pressure him into taking up drugs again.

The treatment was carried out at the island of Shek Kwu Chau, a rocky place lying to the west of HK. An island was chosen so as to lessen the risk of contact with the outside world and the entry of drugs. From the outset, a newly arrived addict received no narcotics but was given methadone as a substitute for a few days whilst he struggled to overcome withdrawal pangs. Thereafter he was put to work. Depending on his skills, it might be helping with domestic jobs, tailoring, carpentry, vegetable growing, animal husbandry, or construction work. It was important to build up his strength and his self-confidence.

Since policy in narcotics was one of the functions of the SCA, I was closely involved in the work of SARDA. The formal opening of the treatment centre at Shek Kwu Chau took place in the early summer in what should have been the wet season. The Governor, Sir Robert Black, a pleasant and efficient man, came by launch on a hot day which otherwise went off without a hitch. The supervisor at the treatment centre was a retired Commander, Royal Navy. Some weeks later, I stayed a couple of nights on the island to learn first-hand how matters were progressing. In the evening on the first day, one of the staff (a Portuguese) came up and said that he did not like the job, wished to leave at once, and wanted his wages up to date. When I pointed out that he was obliged under his contract to give a month's notice of resigning and that no money was kept on the island, he became abusive and threatening. It became apparent that he was unbalanced. He picked up a piece of wood and advanced on the Commander who tried to follow the tradition in the Armed Services of officers doing their physical best to avoid a fight with other ranks. The Commander backed off. I crept up behind the Portuguese, snatched the wood out of his hand, and exchanged an ineffective blow or two. A radio message to the Marine Police brought a launch and the Portuguese was taken into custody. No charge was made, as he was clearly a case for a psychiatric ward.

The dry weather continued. The level in reservoirs began to drop alarmingly, despite water restrictions. The situation became so bad that eventually water in the mains supply was turned on for only four hours every fourth day. It became essential to remember the fourth day and to be on hand at the right time to collect water in containers. Woe betide anyone who forgot. The trick was to learn how to re-use water. This meant that, apart from water in the bathtub, plastic containers should also be filled and a further number left empty. No water was ever allowed to drain away until it had been re-used to the point where it stank. This was where the empty containers came in. They held dirty water to flush the toilet or for other purposes. At weekends, armed with containers, my family and I would go for a swim at a beach, staggering back with loads of sea water for flushing the toilet. The local plastics industry did a roaring business in producing containers. These water restrictions continued for the better part of three thirsty months.

Eddie Teesdale, who had been DO Yuen Long at the time in 1949 when I was first posted as DO Tai Po, was now Colonial Secretary. He organised a system whereby chartered tankers which had cleaned out their tanks sailed up the estuary of the Pearl river to a point beyond the reach of salt water and sucked up the fresh water from the river. This was brought back to a pier at Sham Cheng in the New Territories and pumped into a pipeline to reservoirs. Without this supply, HK might have dried up.

Although not interested in horse racing, I nonetheless accepted invitations on several occasions to the races, largely to find out what it was all about. Being the only form of gambling allowed in HK, horse racing is immensely popular there. It amazed me to see the sophisticated arrangements at the Happy Valley and Sha Tin race courses. Racing was confined to the winter months, with air-conditioned multi-storey stables to combat the heat and humidity of summer. In the centre of the Happy Valley course was a huge TV screen that showed the horses on their way round the track. Before each race, another screen showed the amount of money bet on each horse, with the figures mounting every couple of seconds. Halfway through an afternoon of racing, a queue of people could be seen leaving the race course and discarding betting slips. These were unfortunates who had lost all their money and were sadly making their way home, unwilling even to watch without betting. The lure was gambling, not love of horses in action.

Chapter XXVIII

The Christian concept of a seven-day week with Sunday as a day of rest was traditionally not part of the Chinese calendar which worked only in lunar months. It was Christian missionaries who introduced the idea of the week to China. The original Chinese practice was to work throughout the year except for the main festivals, in particular Chinese New Year when families expected to gather together. It was customary for men to have their hair cut beforehand (barbers usually raised their prices for the period); old clothes and household articles might be replaced; the house would be cleaned; food and flowers were bought for a family feast. In the run-up to the New Year, the abattoirs in HK and Kowloon (both operated then by the Urban Services Department) would slaughter some 15,000 pigs a day compared to the usual 5,000. New Year fairs were crowded with happy visitors looking for sprigs of peach blossom, pots of sweet-smelling jonquils, and bargains of every description.

Those were the days when fireworks and firecrackers were not yet banned in HK. Chinese New Year used to be a period of almost non-stop banging. The object of the crackers was to dispel evil spirits, but in the hands of children crackers tended to be a game for making people jump. It was commonplace for lighted crackers to be thrown from an upper balcony into any rickshaw that happened to be passing below, to the consternation of the passenger. Not only did Chinese New Year sound like a battlefield with the noise of crackers, but the damage from the numerous fires and the injuries caused to people were a constant problem for the authorities.

With several days' holiday at Chinese New Year, it was convenient to make a brief trip to somewhere new, thus escaping the festive turmoil and noise of firecrackers. Margaret and I decided on Kota

Kinabalu in Sabah, as a non-Chinese area likely to be quiet. We did not realise that the town had a large population of Hakka Chinese who kept us awake all night with firecrackers. Furthermore, the hotel turned out to be Chinese-owned and staffed, all away on holiday and their places taken by non-Chinese unfamiliar with the workings of the hotel.

In the Secretariat for Chinese Affairs, I chaired a meeting with the Chief Officer, Fire Brigade, and representatives from the Medical Department and other departments, who agreed that the Government should ban the possession and letting off of all fireworks and firecrackers in HK. Their manufacture in HK was already banned as being too dangerous; the frequent explosion of firework factories in Macao indicated the extent of the danger. When I sent the meeting's conclusions to the Secretariat, I knew that they had no chance of acceptance. It was more than likely that the Secretariat would feel any ban at this juncture might provoke violent public reaction. I guessed correctly. It was several years before the Government felt the public was ready to accept a ban, sweetened by an official annual fireworks display (usually paid for by private enterprise) in the harbour at Chinese New Year.

It is an interesting and important feature of good administration that the common-sense and practical solution to a problem may not be the right answer if it is likely to result in demonstrations and riots. Unless the administration has the majority of the general public behind it, controversial measures that provoke widespread unrest are unwise. Some administrations may go ahead regardless, meeting unrest with repressive measures. But this can be counter-productive because it may alienate the majority of the public and the unrest can be kept in check only if the repressive measures are continued indefinitely. In a democratic regime, no government that acted in this manner could hope to survive the next elections. The trick is for the administration to judge whether reaction to a sensible measure will be widespread or confined to a small minority, possibly noisy beyond its actual size. This is where accurate soundings on the ground and sound political judgment come in. Guesswork is not good enough. A network of official eyes and ears is essential. The Secretariat for Chinese Affairs was part of the network, apart from its traditional role of protecting the interests of the Chinese population.

Leaving aside a belief in the value of following *fung shui*, Chinese traditionally used an almanac called Tung Shing for details of lucky days for various pursuits and propitious times for most aspects of daily and commercial life. Lucky days for weddings meant a rush on the Registry Office, photographers, and restaurants. Few would consider opening a new business or signing a contract without consulting Tung Shing for an appropriate time and date. Teddy Lau Chan-kwok of the Yaumati Ferry Company always arranged to launch his new ferries on a lucky day, at a lucky time somewhere near the practical requirement of high tide.

Fascinated at this arbiter of Chinese life, I arranged to visit the publisher of this almanac, to discover how it was compiled. Did some individual arbitrarily invent these lucky days or was there some logical pattern and system for doing so? In an undistinguished upstairs office, the publisher explained that the almanac had a long history and was originally based on the needs of a rural community. Hence the numerous entries about when to plough, sow and harvest. But the choice of a lucky day lay in examining the relationship between the sun, moon, stars and a few other factors. There was no subjective selection by an individual. A lucky day was nominated by what almost amounted to a scientific process.

The traditional Chinese calendar was a lunar one, with twelve months. For purposes of Chinese New Year, a fictitious thirteenth month provided a month's salary as a bonus for staff. All employees, including Chinese civil servants, expected a bonus at the New Year. But, if at a staff dinner beforehand, the employer served an employee with a chicken wing, it was a traditional gesture to indicate that the employee was about to be sacked. Every year was traditionally ascribed as coming under the influence of some animal (for instance, the Year of the Tiger, the Year of the Rabbit). Each animal endowed children born in that year with particular virtues and habits. It may have been puzzling sometimes for young people to know whether to be themselves or whether to try to measure up to what their particular birth year expected them to be.

Most Chinese appeared to have no difficulty in simultaneously following both the Western calendar and the traditional Chinese one which spoke about the day and the moon (for instance, the 6th day of the 5th moon). For the year, it was commonplace to define it in relation to the reign of a past emperor. In the Secretariat for Chinese Affairs, I was approached one day by a boat-woman who normally rowed a sampan (single oar at the stern) in the harbour, seeking post-registration of the births of her children. She was sturdy, cheerful and illiterate. When I asked her the birth dates of her children, she reeled them all off as the 3rd day of the 4th moon, the 17th day of the 6th moon, etc. Amazed at her apparent memory, I asked how she could possibly remember so accurately. Well, she said, for No. 1 I was rowing across the harbour when the labour pains came on, so the baby was born in the boat. For No. 2, the boat had sprung a leak and was being repaired on shore, so the baby was born in a friend's house. And she detailed the circumstances of each birth in a manner that left no doubt about her truthfulness. It emphasised graphically to me that an illiterate person may have an excellent memory, to make up for being unable to store information in writing.

With three exceptions, Chinese festivals are set by the lunar calendar and therefore vary slightly from year to year. The three exceptions are set by the solar calendar, falling on the same date every year: Lap Chun on 14 February when eggs are supposed to stand on their ends; Ching Ming, the first grave-worshipping festival, on 5 April (or the 6th in leap years); and the winter solstice on 22 December. Most Chinese families celebrated each festival with a large meal that might contain pork, fish and poultry. For certain festivals, chicken is appropriate, for others it is goose. Poultry was usually sold live. (In our early days in Tai Po, Margaret and I bought a live duck in the market and put it in the back of the car for the drive back home. On arrival, the duck was found to be dead, its crop full of sand. As live poultry was sold by weight, it was apparently common practice amongst unscrupulous stallholders to load the birds with sand. Canny customers always felt the crop before buying.)

The post-war construction of multi-storey buildings with high-speed lifts caused me some confusion at first by the traditional Chinese practice of describing the ground floor as the first floor. I found this out only when I went to the wrong floor. But Western influence has virtually driven out this practice. It is an interesting feature that technological advance has to a large extent changed Chinese tradition. Chinese books used to start at what Westerners would describe as the back, with writing in vertical columns from the right-hand top corner of the page. Now most Chinese books follow the Western pattern, with writing across the page from left to right. But horizontal public notices and slogans in Chinese can read from right to left or the other way round. You have to look at the context to know which way to read it.

Where a Chinese letter needed to be sent out from the Secretariat for Chinese Affairs, it would be typed on a Chinese typewriter. This was a lengthy process. Instead of a keyboard with the twenty-six letters of the Western alphabet, there was an associated tray with about 2,000 Chinese characters in silvery metal. The typist had to select the right character from the tray, insert it in the striking arm, print, and then return the character to the tray, to be replaced by the next character. The advent of computers has changed all this. Special computers with Chinese characters have largely taken the place of these typewriters in HK, Singapore, Malaysia, Taiwan and China, whilst Japan and Korea also have their own computers with their particular script.

But computers have not driven out traditional Chinese admiration for good calligraphy, performed with a brush and ink. The Urban Council holds popular exhibitions in the various styles of calligraphy, often in the form of hanging scrolls. In the NT, it was traditional at Chinese New Year to place a scroll of four or six characters on red paper either side of the front doorway. The characters would consist of words denoting happiness, virtue, or good luck. A favourite line was Fragrant Sea, Bright Mountain. For best effect, hanging scrolls tended to be in pairs. Considerable store is still set on traditional Chinese writing with a brush dipped in black ink produced from rubbing an ink stone.

Princess Peter of Greece, who otherwise lived with her husband in Denmark (he was Prince Peter of Greece and Denmark), used to visit HK in the winter, and I was often asked to accompany her on visits to see unusual sights. She and her husband had formerly lived in Kalimpong in Sikkim where they studied anthropology. But they were required to leave there when the Indian Government forced all foreigners out of what it regarded as sensitive border areas. The Princess was interested in aspects of Chinese life. This involved our once sitting through hours of a strange murder trial in the District Court. On another occasion, we visited a Chiu Chau temple on the outskirts of Kowloon Walled City, to see a medium put himself into a trance before lashing his bare back with a spiked ball, followed by lacerating his tongue which he then used to write a Chinese character (for virtue) in blood on a large sheet of white paper. This sort of thing was not in the normal Cantonese way of traditional temple practice.

Chapter XXIX

By this stage in the 1960s, the Government had realised that the former practice of four-year tours for expatriate officers was impracticable, bearing in mind the need for a larger establishment to cope with an officer's nine months' absence on leave. Since air travel was now more extensive, we were offered the option of converting to $2^1/2$-year tours with four months' leave and travel by air. Most of us accepted this option, but a small minority still preferred the sea passage. My next posting was to the Resettlement Department as Assistant Commissioner in charge of estates.

There is a common and understandable belief that the original and main purpose of the Government's resettlement programme was to provide housing for the homeless. This was not the case. As the Communists swept across Nationalist China after the Second World War, reaching Canton in October 1949, refugees poured into HK. Shanty towns sprang up on vacant land, Crown and private. Whole hillsides were taken over, not only for dwelling but also for minor industries. The Government's programme for new schools, medical facilities, water and electrical supplies, roads and recreation was hampered by squatter huts occupying the sites for the proposed facilities. The priority for resettlement was therefore dictated by the urgency of the need for the sites for public development. Once the boundaries of the site for clearance were known, a team was despatched well in advance to survey all structures there, noting the names of occupants and the type of any industry carried on. As soon as the squatters knew of the survey, outsiders tended to rush in with bogus claims and overnight huts. A rapid and accurate survey was essential to avoid cheating.

New resettlement blocks large enough to accommodate all those to be cleared had to be completed in good time before the clearance was due to take place. Each block was required to contain a mix of flats of different sizes to meet the needs of families recorded in the survey. A family of two, three, or four persons needed a flat with the requisite space, and this was calculated on the basis of fourteen square feet per adult. It was not much, but at least the flat provided mains water, electricity, security of tenure and flush toilets. The earliest resettlement blocks were completed in a hurry, with basic facilities and access to rooms via an outside balcony that also doubled as individual kitchens. Inevitably kitchen paraphernalia tended to block the passageway and all rubbish was thrown over the side. Better blocks were later provided and the earliest ones replaced.

Clearances were sometimes traumatic. Squatters in the area to be cleared were told the date for clearance and shown their allocated room which they were free to occupy in advance of clearance. On the due date, a squad of Resettlement labourers moved in with crowbars, pickaxes and saws to demolish any remaining structures which were then removed by lorry and destroyed (to forestall attempts to re-use corrugated iron, etc.). Any squatter who failed to move was evicted and his structure pulled down. This could lead to violence and injury (often to Resettlement staff), for which purpose the Police were always on hand. At one clearance I attended, a recalcitrant squatter armed with a chopper rushed at a Resettlement labourer and had to be restrained.

Life for a tenant in a new resettlement block involved an enormous change. No longer could he spread himself on the hillside, growing a cucumber or creeper on a trellis overhead. Instead he now lived in a concrete box where he or she probably did not know the neighbours; had to struggle up and down stairs or a slow lift to an upper-storey flat; had nowhere for the children to play except in designated playgrounds within the estate where they could not be supervised from the flat; had to put up with possible noise and other nuisance from neighbours; had to stick his laundry out to dry on a bamboo pole projecting from a window. On the other hand, the subsidised rent was low (private landlords were notorious for charging high rents, often with annual increases). There were shops on the ground floor, buses serving the estate, workplaces within reach, and above all security of tenure without the ever-present risk in squatter areas of fire or damage from a tropical storm or typhoon, or landslips and dislodged boulders.

For small industries cleared from squatter areas, multi-storey resettlement factories were provided, catering for an astonishing variety of activities. Apart from the common industries producing plastic bags and thong slippers, small electrical goods, and printing presses, there was a man engaged in turning out gold ornaments and another who produced dental chairs (apparently for use in South-East Asia). Most of these industries had been operated mechanically by hand when in squatter structures. But, on resettlement, they usually upgraded their machinery to operate electrically. This could raise the electrical loading in the resettlement factory enormously, beyond its designed capacity. Every time this happened, the fuses blew and electricity to the entire block was cut off. To avoid this, exasperated tenants would break into the fuse box and replace the fuse with a six-inch nail. This was unacceptably dangerous, as it could lead to fire. The answer was to equip each factory with its own fuse, so that any breakdown in electricity from overloading was confined to the factory concerned, without affecting the remaining tenants in the block. If we had realised in the planning stage that this would happen, individual fuses would have been included initially. But it was something we had to learn from experience.

The Government's resettlement programme continued non-stop over the years, with new problems arising. Overcrowding was one of the biggest. A family of perhaps four persons might have been initially allocated a flat of the appropriate size, but in a couple of years the family may have increased with the birth of more children. Small children of different sexes originally sharing a bedroom grow up and require separate bedrooms. It was apparent that resettling people in a block was not the end of the story. There were continual problems with overcrowding and the need to re-allocate larger flats; failure to pay rent and the reluctance to evict, thus creating another squatter; squabbles between neighbours; the danger to ground-level pedestrians from objects thrown from upper storeys; the occasional case where a tenant had been dead for some time without anyone noticing; attempts at selling or sub-letting the flat in contravention of the tenancy agreement.

At one of our regular meetings with representatives of other departments concerned with resettlement, there was considerable discussion about overcrowding and the need to adopt a formula for a built-in expansion factor in assessing the size of families. The Director of Water Supplies adopted a lighter note by offering to include bromide in the water supply.

Something like half the population of HK lives in government housing, with modest rents. In many cases, more than one member of the family works. There is therefore a fair amount of disposable income in these estates, reflected in the variety of goods and services for sale in resettlement shops, particularly of electrical appliances, beauticians and hairdressers, restaurants, and bookshops. The siting of resettlement estates is crucial. Too far from centres of employment and they will be useless. It is essential that they should be within easy access of work, schools and recreation with plenty of public transport including the Mass Transit Railway (the underground).

Creating sites for resettlement estates was always a problem. Suitable level ground had long since been used for other purposes. The answer was to cut into hillsides, using the fill to form sites. The various branches of the former Public Works Department performed miracles in providing stable sites, with the necessary roads, drainage, electricity and ancillary facilities such as schools, recreation grounds, public libraries, bus stations, refuse-collecting points.

At one stage, fires frequently swept through squatter areas, leaving numbers of homeless. It became apparent that some fires had been deliberately lit in the hopes of jumping the queue of those waiting for resettlement. The answer was to house these homeless people in temporary resettlement areas until such time as their turn came round. It was always a matter of foreseeing irregularity and taking the necessary steps to combat it, better still of being one step ahead.

Chapter XXX

In 1970, I was back in the Defence Branch, in frequent contact with opposite numbers in Headquarters Land Forces and British Forces Headquarters (covering all three Services); both occupying buildings in the pre-war Victoria Barracks area. All the Headquarters buildings have since disappeared and the area is now part of Hong Kong Park. The job was the same routine of combination locks and security, with plenty of paperwork and liaison with the military.

On one occasion I took part as an observer on a Royal Navy frigate together with the Commander British Forces and the Naval Commodore, in a simulated exercise of action to be taken if a Chinese gunboat should enter HK's territorial waters. The RN frigate steamed full speed up to the reported position of the Chinese vessel, with guns trained and ready to fire. I was amazed at this aggressive approach and enquired diffidently of the Commodore what the frigate would be expected to do when it reached the Chinese vessel.

'We'd use the loudhailer and ask them why they were in our waters.'

'But does anyone on board speak Mandarin?' I asked.

'Of course not. We don't carry interpreters.'

There was not much enthusiasm when I suggested that it might be preferable if, on receiving the first report of the presence of a Chinese vessel, the RN called up the Marine Police and arranged for them to approach; they might have Mandarin-speakers and their Chinese crew would in any case speak Cantonese. The frigate could follow the Marine Police launch as back-up. I pointed out that the Chinese vessel might not be deliberately trying to provoke HK. It could for instance be suffering from engine trouble or poor navigation. The essential point was to enquire in Chinese and not to allow matters to develop unnecessarily into a confrontation with possibly political consequences. When

I checked further, it appeared that there was no direct radio link between RN vessels in HK and the RAF, meaning that the frigate could not call directly for an aircraft to shadow the Chinese vessel, but had to rely on relayed messages between the various headquarters in HK. The exercise served a useful purpose in exposing weaknesses that, to my mind, should have been put right long before.

On another occasion in Headquarters Land Forces, we were discussing use of the border road which ran just inside the northern border from Sha Tau Kok in the east to a point in the centre. It appeared that military vehicles patrolled along it regularly. The Colonel in charge of administration looked askance at me when I said that flank marches across the face of the enemy had always been a risky manoeuvre. It would be easy for left-wingers to block the road out of sight round a bend and to do the same behind the patrolling vehicle when it stopped. Bottled up, the vehicle might be in trouble. It seemed that the views of civilians on military matters were not welcome.

This was a time of strained relations with China. From 1950 for the next thirty years, China made clear its distaste for the West and its irritation at Britain's occupation of HK. During this period, the Government and the Police (in particular the Special Branch) carried on a constant struggle to counter communist subversion. Security clearance for staff in sensitive posts was essential, to the dismay of some heads of departments who could not understand why they were discreetly told that X on their staff should not be promoted or posted. The grounds for such action were never disclosed. In many cases, it was because X had relatives in China and so could be blackmailed into doing what the communists told him to do. In a way, the failure to promote saved X from an agonising dilemma. Physical security measures were installed at prime targets for sabotage such as water pumping stations, transport depots, electricity works etc. Europeans who accidentally drifted into China (for instance, yachtsmen) were routinely held on suspicion of being spies. Other Europeans legitimately in China, perhaps on business, were arrested on trumped-up charges and subjected to showpiece trials. The situation reached the point where European civil servants in HK were forbidden by the Government from going to China.

The period of confrontation in 1967 was the most serious. There were incursions and shootings across the border, particularly at Sha Tau Kok where the Police Station was machine-gunned and an armoured car of the Life Guards destroyed. Trevor Bedford, a fellow cadet, was briefly kidnapped on the border. A Police Inspector called Knight was seized and held for some time until he escaped. During the worst of the trouble in 1967, bombs were let off and left-wing mobs surged about. A number of Chinese and Europeans were killed or injured by bomb explosions. Happily the vast majority of the Chinese population of HK (many of them refugees from China) was behind the Government and by no means sympathetic towards the violence and ideology of the left-wingers, particularly as the unrest was bad for local and international business. The staff of the civil service stood firm; an early sign of the population's growing sense of identity with HK and its ready acceptance of a stable government that was not repressive and allowed the individual to get on with making a living.

At the time of confrontation, I was Deputy Director in the Urban Services Department. Some of the staff of the department were understandably worried that left-wingers might be violent towards staff families in the several blocks of departmental married quarters and so apply pressure to persuade the staff to desert the government. I therefore arranged security measures at the quarters and told the Director that I would be visiting there to show that we took the matter seriously. The Director, who was a pleasant fellow but had no military training and was full of strange ideas, told me not to go as it might cause families to think that the directorate was carrying out a fault-finding inspection. I did not argue but quietly ignored his instructions and went anyway, to the evident pleasure of the families that I visited. Man-management was not part of the Director's make-up. Like so many civil servants in those days, he was good at his desk but not in dealing with people.

In the same period of confrontation, whilst visiting a public market on duty, I was approached by a worried stallholder who arranged to see me in my office later with information about a left-wing plot. I therefore got in touch with Special Branch who sent a Chinese Inspector to the interview. The stallholder was agitated in case his identity was disclosed, so I introduced the Inspector as the departmental interpreter (my Cantonese could let me down). Finally, in my car with the stallholder crouching down out of sight, we drove slowly past a market where the stallholder pointed out the agitators. The rest was up to Special Branch.

During the turmoil of confrontation, the rains were late and severe water restrictions had to be applied again for a few weeks, with the same four hours every fourth day that HK had suffered in the 1960s. It was yet another of the black periods that HK and the Government had to weather.

At the end of the Vietnam War, boatloads of Vietnamese, unwilling to accept the new regime in their country, began to arrive in HK and also in other South-East Asian countries. The original refugees were largely ethnic Chinese-speaking Cantonese from the south of Vietnam. Later came a change to ethnic Vietnamese from the north. The two groups did not always get on with each other. The refugees were first housed in a disused godown (shed) in Kowloon Docks where they languished until a decision was reached on what to do with them. On visiting, I remember being struck by the air of resignation and patience shown by whole families sitting around on beds with nothing to do but wait on an official decision about their future. And it was not what they expected. Residents of HK were by no means sympathetic towards the newcomers, fearing that they would compete with locals for housing, education, medical facilities, and jobs. So it was a matter of the HK Government working through the UN High Commission for Refugees to find other countries prepared to accept a quota of Vietnamese refugees. In the meantime, the Vietnamese were moved from camp to camp, sometimes waiting for years before resettlement overseas. But at least they were not at first forcibly sent away in their boats, as apparently happened elsewhere. In the end, by arrangement with Vietnam, the balance were repatriated to that country.

In 1983 on a visit to Macau, I noticed a vessel entering the harbour with the typical outline of a Vietnamese ship and a lot of people on deck. It was intercepted by a Portuguese launch which turned it round and escorted it out in the direction of HK. I had some sympathy with the Macau authorities who, with their limited land area, might have even more problems with boatloads of refugees than did HK.

Chapter XXXI

By now, HK was growing up. There was a growing air of sophistication. The people accepted many Western styles of clothing and way of life. No longer did Chinese girls wear the traditional *cheung sarm*, a tight-fitting dress slit up the legs. A few older matrons might do so and waitresses in some restaurants continued to wear the *cheung sarm*. Blouses and skirts were now commonplace, replaced presently by shirt and trousers. Men were more likely to appear in white shirt and trousers, with leather shoes. Even the shoes have given way to trainers. Hairstyles and grooming have changed. Only a few older women now wear pigtails. The majority have taken to a variety of hairstyles, available in the many hairdressers and beauty shops. Short-back-and-sides for men is almost a thing of the past, with more and more men now sporting long hair and fashionable cuts. Chinese girls who decades ago tended to be as thin as razor blades now have much fuller figures. In the home, electrical appliances became commonplace. Where a family could afford it and had the space, washing machines appeared, likewise electrical sewing machines, rice cookers, hairdryers and curlers, and anything that made life easier. All this was aided by the fact that many families had more than one member earning and adding to the combined income. Furthermore, the many HK clothing factories helped to bring prices down and to provide a wide choice of garments.

In the office, various electrical appliances also appeared: typewriter, photocopier, adding machine, telex (later replaced by fax), computer. The telephone service spread more and more, helped by the fact that there was no charge for internal calls (only an annual fee, irrespective of the number of internal calls). Shopkeepers generally raised no objection to passers-by stopping to use the shop's telephone. Even this practice may have slumped with the widespread ownership of mobile telephones. I can remember my initial surprise at seeing someone using his mobile whilst travelling on the underground Mass Transit Railway (MTR).

Generally Chinese of the modern generation have no difficulty in understanding how to work complicated machinery. Quick to notice things, they can be very observant. A theatre audience can pick up the smallest actions on stage, reacting with laughter or horror.

Football crowds tend to behave in the same manner as Western fans, even to the extent of riotous behaviour inside and outside the stadium if the favourites lose in a needle match. The Urban Services Department learnt to remove all rubbish bins in the vicinity of a stadium before a needle match, and car parking was banned round there too. The popularity of active sport is another phenomenon. Traditionally Chinese did not participate in ball games, which were regarded as activities that made you hot and sweaty like a coolie. This view has given way post-war to a state where games are commonplace: soccer, hockey, tennis, badminton, table tennis. Squash, which used to be regarded as a rich man's pastime, is now a popular sport for both sexes.

The change in attitude has meant a new direction for the Government and the Urban Council which have devoted much attention to the provision of adequate recreation grounds and funds for the various activities. This includes both sports fields and indoor air-conditioned games halls, both evenly spread near residential areas. But there is not much point in providing these facilities if there is not an equal incentive to make full use of them. This has led to the creation of tournaments and competitions, with teams in each, to promote the sport and stimulate constant interest. It is all part of the changing face of HK. The place now is almost unrecognisable from the habits and traditions of fifty years earlier. The spread of concrete has of course transformed HK, Kowloon, and most of all the NT.

In the post-war building boom, a feature that attracted notice for its incongruity was the use of bamboo scaffolding in the construction of modern multi-storey buildings. The speed and skill of the scaffolders were incredible. Vertical and horizontal bamboos were lashed together originally with thin strips of rattan, a bundle of which hung from the scaffolder's belt. In time, the rattan strips were replaced by plastic strips. It was remarkable how the apparently flimsy scaffolding did not topple over, considering that it stood on only one plane with nothing to prop it up. In fact, it was usually tied on to any projection on the side of the building under construction, such as window brackets, outside piping, etc. Latterly, metal scaffolding was introduced, probably as a result of the difficulty and rising expense of obtaining the long bamboo from China and the fact that the bamboo had a limited life for repeated use compared to metal scaffolding. There was a case where, in one street, a building on one side had bamboo scaffolding and on the other side another building had metal scaffolding. A tropical storm caused the metal scaffolding to collapse whilst the bamboo scaffolding held fast.

Pre-war and immediately post-war, building exteriors were finished in plaster which in a few years turned a dingy grey with the effect of rain and damp. Thereafter, finishing tended to be in small mosaic tiles fixed on with cement. But, although the tiles were self-cleaning, the cement round them became discoloured too. The small tiles were replaced in time by large panels of synthetic material like marble, with edges that met closely and left no visible cement. Glass cladding became popular. The exterior of modern multi-storey HK buildings bears no relation to the earlier style, which often had verandahs and pitched roofs. Happily a few of the earlier buildings have been preserved as a reminder of what old HK looked like.

The pace of life in HK has become faster than in many other countries, partly as a result of pressure of increasing population in a limited area. The need to seek a living in a competitive world has also played its part. If you are familiar with the layout of roads in HK, driving a vehicle there may not be the problem that faces motorists driving in HK for the first time and confronted by others with the urge to get ahead. Leave a gap between your vehicle and the one in front and someone is likely to cut in ahead.

Stand back in the crowd awaiting the arrival of a lift and you will be left behind when the lift does arrive. It is usually a matter of every man or woman for himself. I once attended a dinner in a restaurant on the upper floor of a building. At the end of the meal, I joined a crowd in the lift lobby waiting for the lift. Amongst the crowd were a man and a girl, obviously newly married that day and emerging from the celebratory dinner with guests. On the arrival of the lift, the crowd surged forward, with the bridegroom just managing to squeeze in and not a backward glance to his bride who was left behind in the lobby. I wondered whether this unfeeling display boded ill for the success of the marriage or whether it would be accepted as a routine matter of individual initiative, consistent with the general cut and thrust of a driving society.

The illuminated advertising signs in the Central District of HK have to be seen to be believed. The place is a mass of brilliant lines and pictures in all sorts of colours, turning night into day. There is hardly a large office building that is not covered in neon lights top and sides. Looking across the harbour from one side to the other at night can leave a newcomer astounded at the display, and the same applies looking down at the scene at night from up the Peak – provided the Peak is not wreathed in fog. From February to July, the Peak is liable on occasion to be covered in a thick, damp fog that reduces visibility to a few yards. Doors and windows of houses up the Peak are kept closed to exclude the swirling clouds of fog which turn everything mouldy. It used to be the practice to place unused clothes and belongings in a storeroom with a dehumidifier, emptying out surprisingly large amounts of water from the tray. Living up the Peak was cooler and quieter than at lower levels, but it had its problems in summer.

Chapter XXXII

Whilst in the Defence Branch, I was called upon quarterly to change the combination on the Colonial Secretary's safe. He had formerly been Governor of another, smaller colony but was required to step down a rank when posted to the more important territory of HK. It left him nonetheless with something of a grand manner. He was reputed to be less than polite to female secretaries and others if they did not stand up for themselves. On one occasion as I was working on his safe, he distracted me so that I did something wrong and for the moment was stumped about how to put it right. I dared not tell him that I had jammed the combination with the safe door open. Presently he enquired testily why I was taking so long and was not reassured by my airy reply. I continued to fiddle frantically and was rewarded eventually by getting things right again.

One Sunday morning, he telephoned me at home to instruct me to go to his office in the Secretariat and collect some pills from his desk drawer. He felt it necessary to explain that he would not drive himself in his car, as it would be awkward for the Colonial Secretary to be involved in an accident, nor was he willing to require his driver on his day of rest to take him in the official car. (But it was apparently all right to ask me on my day of rest. Previous CSs had never worried about driving their own cars.) This errand meant my driving from my quarters on the Peak to the Secretariat building, getting the watchman to let me in, opening the two combination locks on the outer Defence Branch door, unlocking the inside grille door, unlocking my office door, opening my combination safe, extracting the duplicate key to the door of the CS's office, and then closing everything again. Unfortunately, in my haste, I forgot to bring the key to my office door and therefore had to drive home again to fetch it. This wasted half an hour, during which time the CS telephoned my wife to enquire why I was taking so long. Eventually, I retrieved and delivered the pills which sadly did not choke him.

I once appeared before the Executive Council in connection with proposed regulations that would exempt male and female Sikhs from the requirement to wear the prescribed crash helmet whilst riding a motorcycle. I explained that Sikhs were obliged by their religion not to wear any form of headgear other than a turban and that, even in the Second World War, Sikhs in the Forces were exempt from wearing steel helmets. At this, the CS stepped in to say that this was not the case and that they had always worn steel helmets. Luckily I was able to stop myself flatly contradicting him in front of the Governor and Executive Councillors.

The official winter uniform for the Governor consisted of a dark blue woollen jacket and trousers with a cocked hat and a sword. It did not look too bad on the occasions when the Governor wore it for parades and suchlike, although it could have been much improved. It had the air of something theatrical from the turn of the century. It was frankly out of date and tended to make one embarrassed rather than impressed. The official summer uniform was worse. Made of a drill cotton, there was a high-collared white jacket and tight white trousers with a strap that passed under the black boots. Topped by a white spiked helmet, the outfit was completed by a sword that passed through a hole in the trousers, making it difficult to sit down. This was apparently a uniform designed for tropical Africa and applied regardless to all Britain's colonial territories. It was also the official uniform for the Colonial Administrative Service. As it was not obligatory in HK, I declined to purchase or wear one. But some fellow cadets did, appearing in this uncomfortable uniform at their weddings and on other official occasions.

Paul Tsui, the first Chinese cadet, told me once that, whilst he was District Officer Yuen Long, he used to wear the uniform at official openings, largely to distinguish himself in an otherwise Chinese throng. On one occasion, in summer at an open-air ceremony attended by local dignitaries and senior military officers, it had suddenly poured with rain. Paul, along with everyone else, raced for cover. Unfortunately he slipped on wet earth and fell headlong into a muddy pool in his white uniform. To add insult to injury, his false teeth came out.

Paul was a sturdy individual. During the confrontation of 1967, the communists classed him as a running dog with the British administration and therefore a traitor. He was placed on a death list. Trailed everywhere for weeks by protective Police, Paul was unworried by the death threat.

Chapter XXXIII

Hong Kong is now so built-up, with development spreading further and further afield, that it is difficult to imagine that it ever had any wildlife. But it did. In early 1949, there was a newspaper report of a village woman cutting grass in the NT and encountering a tiger (or leopard) which she fended off with her sickle; it was presumably not a serious attack. There had apparently been several pre-war reports of similar encounters when tigers had ranged as far south as the NT in winter. There used to be a stuffed tiger's head displayed in the Central Police Station. Sometime around the First World War, the animal had killed one or more policemen hunting it in the NT.

In the summer of 1949 or 1950, the English language *South China Morning Post* carried an article about a Constable on a Marine Police launch anchored offshore in Tolo harbour on the west side of the Sai Kung peninsula. The Constable reported to the European Inspector on board that there was a large snake on the foredeck. The Inspector doubted this and was surprised to find a python coiled up there. It had apparently swum from the shore (possibly to cool off from the summer heat), climbed the anchor chain, and dozed off on the deck.

Although most HK residents never see a snake (most species are nocturnal), there were reports of snakes turning up from time to time in the most unlikely places. At one stage in the 1960s, we lived temporarily up the Peak in a house with garden whilst its usual occupant was away on leave. After the grass and undergrowth had been cut from beneath a hedge in the garden, a cobra that apparently lived there must have been disturbed, because Margaret met it shortly afterwards slithering up the steps trying to get into the house.

Walking once in winter in the Saikung district of the NT with my young family, I came round a corner to meet a cobra on the path. It was as surprised as myself and immediately reared up, spread its hood, hissed loudly, and moved threateningly towards me. I backed off, calling out 'Snake' and retreating into small pushing bodies that shoved forward crying 'Where, where? I want to see.' There was some unseemly confusion, relieved only when the cobra decided to slip away having made its point.

One day, from our upper-storey flat in Homestead Road, the Peak, I saw a six-foot snake making its way along the lawn downstairs. A couple of experts from the Pest Control Section came to deal with it. The snake meanwhile had slipped into a covered surface channel and remained there. So newspaper and sulphur powder were lit at one end of the drain and fanned towards the snake which duly emerged in a hurry at the other end, to be scooped up with a noose at the end of a pole and be popped into a canvas bag for release elsewhere in the country. The Pest Control Section never killed the snakes it caught (unless circumstances left no option), but always released them into the wild, particularly in the case of this rat snake which would help the Section in its task of keeping down the population of rats.

Inevitably in a large and crowded city like HK, with squalid areas awaiting development, rats flourished enormously. Breeding prolifically, they were cunning and bold. John Romer, the Pest Control Officer in the Urban Services Department, was an expert on most forms of wildlife. He waged a relentless war on rats, emphasising to architects and city planners that the first step was to ensure that building plans left no scope for rats to hide or enter premises. For instance, if outside pipes on multi-storey buildings were placed only inches away from the wall, a rat could easily climb by bracing its back on the pipe and its feet on the wall. Pipes must either be placed internally or well away from the outside wall. No hollows should be left between the backs of cupboards and the wall; cupboards must back on to the wall itself.

In a city port like HK, there used to be an ever-present risk of bubonic plague carried by fleas on rats. To check on the possible presence of these fleas, the Pest Control Section provided small, green-painted bins secured on lamp standards throughout residential areas.

Residents were encouraged to place their trapped dead rats in the bins, in the Jeyes fluid at the bottom. The bins were emptied daily and a random selection of the rats checked for infected fleas. After many years of unsuccessful checking and a WHO announcement that bubonic plague had been eradicated, the rat bins were later discontinued. But for years, the rat bins had been a standard feature of the HK scene. Daily disposal of the dead and soaking-wet rats was a messy problem, requiring a fierce fire in pits sited well away from the urban areas to avoid nuisance from the oily and smelly smoke. When refuse incinerators were introduced, the dead rats were thankfully dumped in with the refuse (likewise seized narcotics) for disposal.

In the 1950s, when Blake Pier in HK was still a wooden structure (since replaced by a concrete one), there was a newspaper article about a group of men indulging in the common practice of fishing from the pier with handlines. Startled by feeling the pier shaking, the fishermen investigated to find a whale rubbing itself against the wooden uprights, presumably to remove marine growth from its skin.

In the 1960s, and 1970s, when I lived in various places up the Peak, it was commonplace to hear barking deer at night barking on the hillside, usually in the wooded catchment areas above the Aberdeen and Pok Fu Lam reservoirs. If you were lucky, you might see one in daylight in the Cape D'Aguilar area. Now there are hardly any left in HK and certainly not to be heard barking. Illegal hunting and attacks by dogs have almost wiped them out. Pre-war residents of the Peak told me that their vegetable gardens were always fenced in to exclude barking deer and porcupines which overnight could clear beds of lettuce, etc. Only once was I able to see a live porcupine, caught in the headlights of the car at night as it crossed the road.

In about 1961, John Romer was given a ferret-badger, a brown and white mammal about a foot long, caught by Chinese staff of the Queen Mary Hospital on the Pok Fu Lam hillside. I remember John showing it to me in a cage in the Pest Control office before it was donated to the London Zoo where I saw it again later. At about the same time, John was given a live monitor lizard which was about a yard long. He was then living in a hostel in Upper Albert Road where he invited me to see it, in his bathroom. He expertly grabbed it by the back so as to avoid its formidable claws. It too was sent elsewhere, if only to allow John to use his bathroom for its proper purpose. The lizard had been caught originally by workers in a quarry near Kwun Tong.

Up till about the 1970s, a group of monkeys (long-tailed macaque) lived in the area between the old Tai Po Road and the Shing Mun reservoir, having probably been released from captivity during the Pacific War. This species is not indigenous to HK. The group could often be seen at the side of the road where motorists would sometimes stop and feed them.

Hunting for wild boar used to take place in the 1950s in the NT but, with disturbance of habitat and a lack of wild pig, it has died out. I remember seeing a dead boar strapped to the front of a hunter's car in Tai Po Market. At about that time, there was a newspaper report of an army wife walking in the Tai Po Kau forestry reserve and being injured by a wild boar that had been wounded (but not killed) by a hunter higher up the hill.

There are – or were – at least thirty-five species of wild mammals in HK, most of them nocturnal and by this time probably few and far between. There must be very few HK residents who have ever seen a wild pangolin (scaly anteater), or one of the three species of civet, or a Chinese otter, or a fox, or a mongoose, or a badger.

On the other hand, many more HK residents are aware of the presence of birds, most of which are diurnal and more readily seen. For birdwatchers, the territory provides excellent opportunities, particularly in winter when all sorts of birds from chilly North China and Siberia migrate south through HK or spend the winter there in warmer weather. The exposed mud of Deep Bay (which is, in fact, quite shallow) and the Mai Po marshes provide excellent feeding grounds for waders and water birds, whilst the several woods, vegetated hillsides and paddi fields offer suitable habitat for a range of cuckoos, flycatchers, robins, chats, warblers and buntings.

It used to be said that there were only two things that a Chinese would do with a wild bird: eat it or put it in a cage. Whilst this may still be true up to a point, there is now a welcome trend towards conservation through the efforts of the World Wide Fund for Nature (HK) and the HK Birdwatching Society.

It was in the 1970s that the Government, through the efforts of Sir Jack Cater, Chief Secretary (the designation Colonial Secretary had at long last been changed to Chief Secretary), legislated to provide a series of country parks, consisting mostly of undeveloped hillsides and valleys. Something like 40 per cent of the territory became Country Parks, increasingly popular with young people hiking and camping at weekends and holidays. Car parks and barbecue places at vantage points could be crowded out at times, with families enjoying an outing in the country. The fact that many people never stirred farther than 100 yards from their vehicles was immaterial; in some ways an advantage, as it ensured litter was not scattered too widely. The popularity of country parks was yet another instance of changing public attitudes and of meeting people's growing expectations. I was surprised at a dinner party when my neighbour, an elegant sophisticated young Chinese lady who looked as if she kept in close touch with a beauty parlour, said that she frequently went camping with her family in the NT.

Chapter XXXIV

It may be thought that, in a large and crowded city like HK with miles of commercial and residential skyscrapers, residents must lead an entirely urban life, surrounded by the noise of the traffic, radios, air-conditioners and people. To an extent this is true. But it is still possible to escape much of this. The government and the Urban Council have over the years provided a string of parks, playgrounds and recreation areas, catering for active and passive interests, and sited conveniently close to centres of population. But providing these facilities is of little use if not promoted. It is also necessary to encourage people by creating competitions and tournaments, with visiting teams to stimulate that extra push for excellence. This has had its effects.

In the decade or so after the Pacific War, the people of HK were too busy struggling to make a living and to establish new roots to have time or energy to spare on sport. Thereafter increasing affluence, better housing and a growing sense of identity and freedom allowed residents to find time for leisure and the pursuit of recreation. Football became a popular pastime among young men in winter. Both sexes took to badminton and table tennis which could be played throughout the year, especially in the air-conditioned games halls provided by the Urban Council. In summer, local swimming pools could be crowded. Children's playgrounds contained all sorts of equipment designed to attract and stretch children in healthy exercise. For retired citizens, there were parks with trees, shrubs and water features to relax the mind and provide shade from the hot sun. Knots of elderly people might be seen round tables and chairs, playing Chinese checkers or chatting happily.

All this was in contrast to the educated pre-war Chinese attitude of not taking exercise that made one hot and sweaty like a coolie (anglicised term for the Cantonese *'gwoo lay'*, meaning bitter sweat). Better-off Chinese now played tennis and golf, sailed their yachts and cabin cruisers, went swimming and horse-riding. There was a complete change of attitude, with increased expectations of what was needed to achieve a satisfying life. Not all, of course, could reach this point. To many, life was still a struggle, spent largely working in an office or shop and in a cramped flat.

In the former Kai Tak airport, it was common to see Chinese children racing up and down the large reception hall, dodging round groups of people. At first, the children's excitement puzzled me until I realised that, brought up in a perhaps upper-storey flat, they had seldom come across a large space where they could run about. By contrast, at a country park one day, a young mother showed much concern at her son's attempts to scramble up a steep bank. The lad was delighted to be adventurous, whereas the mother, who presumably had lived all her life in the city, had apparently no experience of this sort of thing and was clucking in horror at what her son was doing. The increasing opportunities in HK for more strenuous pursuits may help to break down any tendency to produce a soft and indolent generation.

For those more interested in the arts, the field is wide open in encouraging both Western and Chinese music, painting, dance, film and literature. By providing central and local venues for concerts and productions, the Urban Council has stimulated a demand, helped by the import of visiting international companies and artistes. Low and subsidised admission prices for students ensured new generations of concert-goers. A network of public libraries, with equal demand for Chinese and English sections, was always full, with sections for reference books, adults books (not the naughty sort), children's books, music listening, and a students' study room. When it was found, years ago, that students were taking up too much room in the libraries doing their school homework, special rooms for the purpose were set up. Demand was such that a booking system had to be introduced. It was all a result of lack of quiet space in cramped domestic flats (Cantonese tend to be noisy people; a street full of people in Beijing can be quieter than one in HK). At one stage, something like 75 per cent of the users of HK's public libraries were schoolchildren anxious to broaden their minds. It could almost be said that the public libraries were part of the educational system.

The same is partly true of the Museum of Art, the Museum of History and the Science Museum. From its outset, the Museum of Art concentrated on the material of South China, purchasing from local sources and at the twice-yearly Sotheby's auctions in HK. The aim was to obtain a good representative selection of material from each stage of development in the fields of ceramics, bamboo, jade, bronze and fine art. Whether you liked the particular picture or bowl was immaterial. The need was to bridge gaps in the stages of development of that particular field of art, so that students and artists in that field could observe and learn.

The Museum of History gathered material from the early days of HK and from further back. Its popular permanent exhibition, 'The Story of HK', showed the earliest-known human activities in the area, the structure of its rural society, clan organisation, and subsequent development to become a major metropolis. Both museums attracted school visits, and others interested in Chinese culture and the origins of HK. Even more school visits were made to the Science Museum which encouraged children to try out machines and gradually learn something of science and how things work. The more noise a machine made when operated and the more lights that flashed, the more popular it became. Before the actual premises for the Science Museum were built, there had been a curator who for two or more years had no museum and only a handful of exhibits, all stored. He spent his time encouraging private companies to sponsor equipment and material, planning the layout of the proposed building, and pressing for the required item in the priority list of the public works programme. One could only sympathise with his sense of frustration. As with so many things in HK, all wanting to be done at the same time, a priority list based on convincing criteria was essential to keep within the limits of the money and resources available.

The main point is that, although outsiders may think that the people of HK live only for trade and commerce, immersed in the pursuit of money, this was far from the case. Many took a profound interest in the arts, helped by the provision of facilities for viewing and enjoying them. It is true to say that the provision of a good public facility to some extent tends to generate its own demand. If it was not there, it might not be generally missed. But put it there and promote it, and people will patronise it, as if it were a newly opened restaurant. Several leading Chinese and Western businessmen were patrons of the arts, having the wealth to obtain Chinese artifacts and the expertise to judge the good from the bad or from fakes. The Urban Council invited some of the experts to form a voluntary panel to advise on the acquisition of material from individuals and at auctions, including the estimated value and the bona fides of their provenance (no purchases of articles from shady sources). The opinions of these experts were invaluable. Objective and unselfish, they served HK well and laid the foundations of the magnificent collections in the various museums.

Carrying matters further in the years 1976 to 1983 when I was Director of Urban Services, I used to invite leading Chinese collectors to Chinese dinners to persuade them to donate their collections to a museum, so as to avoid the collections being eventually split up piecemeal when the collector passed away. It was seldom the case that the family wished to keep the collection. I emphasised that, after the collector had spent a lifetime amassing his pieces, it was a pity to allow them to disperse, thus denying HK people the opportunity to see them. In most cases, collectors were unwilling to commit themselves in advance but usually indicated that, if they did agree to donate, their material must be placed in a separate gallery under their name and well away from any other inferior material. This was easily accepted, with assurances that the museums displayed only material of international class. Second-rate material was not displayed, although in some cases a slightly flawed or chipped article might be purchased cheaper at auction if it was otherwise an excellent specimen and filled a gap in the collection.

An important part of each museum was its conservation section. In the Museum of Art, the conservator was kept busy cleaning pictures, checking background with a thermo-luminescence machine, repairing ceramics with special glue that did not discolour with age, treating bronze against bronze disease, and generally keeping material in good condition. In the Museum of History, the conservator might be required to treat wooden material against woodworm or rot, leather against cracking, metal against rusting, and anything that was liable to come apart. As material aged, its maintenance became of greater importance, with the need to control temperature and humidity.

The late K.S. Lo, whom I knew at that time only slightly, approached me one day offering to donate his collection of Chinese teaware to the Museum of Art, provided it was displayed separately in Flagstaff House. This building, dating from 1846, had for many years been the official residence of the Commander, British Forces, but had latterly reverted to the Government. The offer was gladly accepted, with the Government happy to find a worthwhile use for this historic building. It was restored to its original state and now houses K.S. Lo's magnificent collection, in a fine setting on a headland overlooking the harbour, at the side of HK Park.

One of the more interesting aspects of the cultural side of HK was the unexpected depth of talent in English-speaking amateur dramatics and singing, often of a truly professional standard. Over the years, most of the Gilbert and Sullivan operettas were performed, together with popular productions like *Orpheus in the Underworld*. It was always a surprise to recognise a colleague holding forth lustily in *The Gondoliers* or acting as the wicked ogre in pantomime. And the cast usually contained Chinese too.

Chapter XXXV

From 1971 to 1975, I was Commissioner for Transport at a time when there was a surge of public interest in measures to reduce increasing traffic congestion and to provide better public transport which was in the hands of three private companies: the Kowloon Motor Bus Company covering Kowloon and the NT; the China Motor Bus Company covering HK island; and the Tramway Company which ran a service with overhead wires from east to west along the waterfront of HK island. As the bus companies pointed out, traffic congestion was so bad that buses could not run to schedule, and there was unfair competition from the hordes of *pak pai* (private cars illegally plying for hire as taxis, with passengers unwilling to testify in court). The trams were old, had no stop lights (they operated on DC current which precluded it), tended to obstruct traffic, and tram stops were in the middle of the road (with passengers having to run the gauntlet of traffic to get to and from the roadside pavement). But trams carried more passengers between destinations than buses. There could be no question of getting rid of them, as had been the case in other cities.

The bus companies were encouraged and persuaded to sharpen their schedules, maintain their buses better and provide improved conditions for staff. Financially, they saved on salaries by making their buses one-man-operated, in place of the former wasteful practice of employing a conductor to collect fares. Buses soon began to carry eye-catching advertisements on the sides, causing one to forget that in earlier days there had been nothing but red paint all over them.

Kowloon and the urban areas of HK island had developed as virtually two separate cities, divided by nearly a mile of sea and linked at the narrowest point by the private Star Ferry Company, which ran an efficient and speedy passenger service. The HK and Yaumati Ferry Company also ran competent ferry services for passengers and vehicles between different points on the HK and Kowloon waterfronts, and also to outlying islands. Yet another private company operated ferries between HK island and Macau. It was becoming abundantly clear to traffic engineers in the Public Works Department and to the Transport Department that a vehicular connection linking HK and Kowloon was essential. A bridge was ruled out as a possible obstruction to shipping and because of the serious effects that typhoon winds might have on the structure and vehicles. The better alternative was a tunnel. Accordingly, a contract was let for a private consortium, at its own expense, to build, maintain and operate a cross-harbour toll tunnel. The tunnel was built in sections that were lowered into prepared beds below the sea floor, with a covering of soil to avoid ships' anchors fouling the tunnel. The necessary network of roads at each end of the tunnel was provided by the Government, and woe betide any motorist who, in the cut and thrust of HK traffic, took the wrong turning; they could end up in Kowloon by mistake.

The effect on traffic was dramatic, and equally so in allowing the workforce to move more easily by public transport through the tunnel from their home on one side of the harbour and their work on the other. On the other hand, it tended to draw a lot of traffic to the two tunnel ends, and emphasised the eventual need to provide further cross-harbour vehicular tunnels east and west of the original central one.

As far as traffic congestion was concerned, the Road Traffic Advisory Committee of which I was chairman gave a lot of thought to the usual measures commonplace today, such as one-way streets, clearways, off-road bus stops, fly-overs, underpasses, elevated roads, bus lanes, box junctions. Gradually matters improved, and the Police were able to make some progress in combatting the incidence of *pak pais*. In my regular meetings with the representatives of the Taxi Drivers Association, the continual criticism and complaints died down to the point where I was able to persuade them to agree to a standard livery for taxis to make them easily recognisable at a distance. Hence the current silver upperwork and red lower part of the taxi body, with an illuminated TAXI sign on top in English and Chinese.

The Transport Department, when I first started there, was housed in a pre-war building in Wanchai that had previously been part of HMS Tamar, the former naval shore establishment. It was almost the only government department that did not have its own departmental car for conveying staff on duty to and from meetings. I therefore normally travelled by tram to attend meetings in the government secretariat. Returning by taxi one day, the taxi driver was at first reluctant to take me to the Transport Department, saying that I had better watch my step there as the man in charge was a wicked devil. I promised to be careful.

On another occasion, returning in my own car from Lau Fau Shan in the northern part of the NT, the car suffered a puncture. When I put on the spare tyre, it proved to be so under-inflated as to be useless. I therefore stood on the side of the road and waved down a private car driven by a Chinese lady. Explaining my predicament, she told me to get into the car which already had a couple of children in the back and, declining my help, put the punctured tyre in the boot of the car. Off we went to Yuen Long where she told me she must first deliver the children back to their home. The car was a *pak pai* which provided a daily service taking these particular children to and from school. The woman's kindness and frank account of how she made a modest livelihood by a reliable daily service was an eye-opener to the way by which so many HK people survived. She went further by taking me to a tyre-repair shop which dealt with the puncture in its workshop (the area of pavement outside the actual shop) whilst she waited and chatted, and then delivered me back to my car. I was so grateful that I paid her almost enough to buy a new car. She never knew, of course, who I was or that it was really my duty to report her to the Police. This was an occasion to turn a blind eye.

The opening of the cross-harbour tunnel was a splendid occasion, with invited guests assembling at the Kowloon end and finally going through the tunnel in a fleet of rickshaws. This was easy going in the first half of the tunnel which sloped down from the portal, but my puller ran out of breath and was unable to proceed in the second, uphill stage. I therefore walked the remainder and was in good appetite at the official luncheon afterwards in the Hilton Hotel. Margaret was seated beside me, with Mr Li Ka-Shing, a leading property developer, on her right. Mr Li spent part of the meal hurrying to and from the telephone (happily no mobiles in those days), no doubt attending to business deals. At one stage, Margaret remarked to him what a magnificent meal was provided. 'Thank you very much,' said Mr Li. 'I own this hotel.'

Not all residents were happy with traffic re-arrangements. There was considerable public criticism and demands for a return to the status quo. It was necessary to stand firm and patiently counter erroneous claims by pointing out their errors. I found myself conducting a continual series of public relations exercises through letters to the Press, talks to organisations, radio and television interviews. The demands of the publicity media seemed insatiable. One irate resident of Mid-Levels on HK island, who objected to the introduction of a one-way traffic system past his block of flats, allowed his feelings to run riot with remarks about my behaving in a high-handed manner like a medieval baron, complete with *droit de seigneur*. I looked this up in government regulations, but alas there was no such fringe benefit.

In an interview, a newspaper demanded to know why I complained about the waste of road space taken up by private cars containing only the driver but yet drove my own car to and from my office. When I said that this was not the case and that I took the bus daily from the Peak (anticipating this criticism), I was pressed for details of the bus and its time of departure. Next morning, to my surprise, there was a reporter and photographer waiting for me at the bus stop, with a favourable article next day.

Although much had been done to reduce traffic congestion and to control the number of additional vehicles (by higher vehicle licence fees) on the limited network of roads, more needed to be done to make it easier for people to travel. In other words a different form of public transport was needed, avoiding surface conflict with traffic lights, vehicles, and the weather. An underground railway was the obvious answer. To this end, research was conducted on estimated passenger movement and volume in different urban districts, so as to map out a possible route of what came to be known as the MTR (Mass Transit Railway). A traffic engineer visited almost every known underground railway in the world to gather information about what to plan for and what to avoid. Contracts were let, and HK suffered years of inconvenience as roads were dug up and sections closed off. Despite the inevitable teething troubles, the final result was a masterpiece, with the self-financing MTR Corporation running smoothly without loss and huge numbers of daily passengers. Tickets in stations are sold only by machine. Stations and carriages are air-conditioned. Carriages contain five double doors to allow rapid entry and exit. Materials and equipment were all of top quality to ensure future trouble-free maintenance.

The Transport Department operated vehicle inspection centres on either side of the harbour, for six-monthly inspection of taxis and their meters; of buses and new makes that the bus company wished to import; of commercial vehicles; and of vehicles involved in accidents where the Police might need technical evidence.

The driver testing section conducted practical driving tests for applicants seeking the issue of driving licences. This section became overloaded, with the result that appointments for tests had to be set further and further ahead. The more this occurred, the more people began to rush forward to book tests. Most of them did not own cars but wanted a licence as a useful aid to seeking employment. I organised a crash test programme (an unfortunate choice of words), employing any civil servant with a driving licence prepared to work at weekends and in the evenings as an auxiliary driving test examiner. A letter addressed to me caused some surprise by wanting to book a test a few years hence (delays were not really that bad). I understood the position when I looked at the sender's address: HM Prison, Stanley.

Another letter came from an unhappy individual who said that he had taken the test six times, failing each time. He was convinced that the examiners were in league against him and that he was really a competent driver. In case there was any irregularity, I turned up unannounced at this man's next test, to the surprise of the examiner who was mollified only when I sat in the back of the car and promised not to say a word. It was only too obvious in the course of the test that the applicant was a hopeless driver, liable to be a menace on the road if licensed. When it came to the point of his doing a three-point turn in the road, he became so disorganised that the examiner failed him forthwith and took over the wheel, with me standing outside in a blinding shower of rain guiding him in turning the vehicle. The episode put paid to the allegations.

Chapter XXXVI

Before I joined the Transport Department, I was aware of allegations that some of its staff were corrupt. There were suggestions that the issue of driving licences could be arranged and that various other irregularities were happening. This was a time of heightened public and official awareness of corruption and of the need to take effective steps to combat it. The Anti-Corruption Branch of the Police was finding the task too much. The corrupt activities of individuals were bad enough, but infinitely worse was syndicated corruption whereby a whole section of staff, from senior to junior, was on the take, and anyone not prepared to join found himself pushed out of the way, with no one at the top prepared to listen to his complaints. The extent of the cover-ups masked the true and serious state of corruption, centring largely on gambling, prostitution and drugs, but also extending to the issue of licences or permits, building plans and any exercise of discretion.

In the Transport Department, I began by issuing a comprehensive set of departmental instructions, on the principle that it is useless to tell a member of staff that he is doing the wrong thing if you have not first laid down what is the right thing. Disciplinary proceedings would get nowhere without clear rules to point to. Gradually things improved in the department and we were able to hold our heads up. At the same time, the Governor, Sir Murray MacLehose, introduced the Independent Commission Against Corruption (ICAC) under Sir Jack Cater. A Target Committee consisting of officials and unofficials decided the priority of targets, weeding out frivolous and malicious allegations. With its own staff, the Commission did its own investigation and prosecution. This was the essence of its independence. There was no question of handing over bits and pieces of responsibility to the Police, Legal Department, or elsewhere, with the risk of delay, obstruction or contrary views. The one authority was responsible throughout (Australian States have yet to realise this).

The spectacular success of the ICAC in reducing the incidence of corruption, in particular of syndicated corruption, was heart-warming. But this is not to say that corruption thereafter ceased to occur. It still continued on a smaller scale and required continuing vigilance. The publicity campaign waged by the ICAC succeeded in educating the public to what constitutes corruption (forbearing to do one's duty in return for money or money's worth) and in winning the public over to the point of view that a corrupt person is acting against the public interest and should be reported (anonymous allegations were always acceptable).

It was sometimes an eye-opener to discover that colleagues whom one had worked with were prosecuted for corruption. There appeared to be no obvious pattern of character for an outsider to judge whether a person was liable to be corrupt. Europeans were just as liable as Chinese, and women as much as men. It was by no means the case that only low-salaried persons stooped to corruption. Quite a few of the better-off were corrupt too, presumably giving way to greed. A European civil servant of middling seniority who lived near me up the Peak and whose children often played with mine simply did not return from leave in Europe, no doubt feeling that he had made enough and wished to avoid detection.

For a European (and possibly also for Chinese), HK was full of temptations: alcohol, women, narcotics, money, position, power. It took strength of character to tread the right path at all times. It could be fatal to stray once or twice, breaking the ice and finding that it was not so bad after all and could be done again. This might lead to deceiving oneself into thinking that there was no real harm in it. At that point, you were already lost.

Some years earlier, whilst in the Secretariat for Chinese Affairs, I had given talks a couple of times to newly-appointed expatriate officers on induction courses, about the Chinese way of life. Apart from the obvious traits, such as that Chinese usually preferred a consensus of views rather than a majority decision, I emphasised that, for an expatriate, it was necessary to acquire and retain throughout one's service a due sense of humility and to avoid any tendency towards arrogant superiority. This was greeted in silence. I sensed some disbelief, as if I was a hot-gospeller addressing an atheist.

Amongst civil servants, in considering draft legislation, new procedures and ideas, it became standard practice to check the material for loopholes that could be exploited by the corrupt. This checking needed to be done with experienced and wide-open eyes by those who knew the sort of thing that could be turned to irregular advantage. It was only too apparent that the corrupt were quick to notice loopholes and to exploit them on the quiet. I was once told by the Attorney General of an Australian State that 'there is no evidence of corruption here', as if corrupt persons were going to wave a flag to draw attention to themselves. A well-meaning person, he was clearly out of his depth and did not understand that the essence of a corrupt system is to carry on in complete secrecy.

Chapter XXXVII

The Convention of Peking 1898 – by which China agreed to lease the NT to Britain for 99 years – also allowed the Mandarin in Kowloon Walled City to continue functioning as a sort of magistrate and local authority within the city walls. But the Convention unfortunately did not make it clear whether the Walled City was Chinese or British territory, nor whether the arrangements applied only to the Mandarin alive in 1898 or to his successors as well. Up till the outbreak of the Pacific War in 1941, the HK Government played safe by keeping out of the Walled City which seemed to manage adequately on its own. The invading Japanese in the Pacific War had no such compunctions. They tore down the city walls in order to extend the inadequate Kai Tak airport. Now only a tiny part of the original wall remains, preserved in a small amenity plot near the former airport.

Post-war the Government's hands-off policy towards the Walled City began to prove awkward, as more and more illegal activities found a relatively safe haven there. Unless pursuing known perpetrators of serious crime such as murder, the Police generally kept out, likewise staff of other government departments. The situation was aggravated after 1949 by fears that government action within the Walled City might cause the Chinese authorities to claim jurisdiction there. But public health and other issues such as fire forced the Government to step in gradually. Much of the area lay below the level of the surrounding developed parts and was therefore subject to flooding. As there was only surface drainage, flood water had no proper outlet. With no official refuse collection, garbage piled up everywhere in stinking heaps, breeding flies and rats. (I once saw a woman there, trying to dispose of a rat trapped in a cage by lighting newspaper under the cage). Electricity wires trailed all over the place in illegal connections, likewise water pipes often from wells absorbing the filthy surface water. Multi-storey buildings constructed without regard to building regulations sprouted up, prompting the Government at one stage to insist on the removal of some upper storeys that projected above the safe height for aircraft approaches to Kai Tak Airport. Dark lanes, sometimes so narrow that two persons could hardly pass each other, led everywhere. At the edge of the Walled City fronting on to Carpenter Road was a row of unregistered dentists, where you could watch people in dental chairs having gold or brass fillings put in their teeth.

After a couple of serious fires in the Walled City, it was eventually agreed that the Urban Services Department in which I was then serving should undertake the removal of refuse and nightsoil in there. This was not easy, as it is impracticable to attempt to sweep unpaved areas. The best that could be done was to clean out surface channels, set up rubbish bins and construct a temporary latrine, with pails emptied daily. Residents welcomed the facilities and asked for more. On one visit of inspection with a Police escort, we stopped at a dingy structure carrying a handwritten Chinese notice pinned to a locked door and saying something to the effect that, since there were Police in the vicinity, business was temporarily suspended but would resume after the Police had left. It was obviously a narcotics den.

On another visit, which for some reason included a couple of senior army officers, we had a look at the temporary latrine. To get in, we had to step over the dead body of an emaciated Chinese man, disturbing a mass of flies. The architect with us turned green. 'Not steady under fire' murmured one of the officers. The latrine attendant explained to me that numerous drug addicts made use of the latrine for a fix. Nearly every day there was a body of some unfortunate there. He may have died elsewhere in the Walled City but had been brought to the latrine, knowing that the USD would remove the body and arrange its burial or cremation.

The squalor in the Walled City was appalling and a disgrace to the Government, which was caught in a dilemma. If it took strong action, it would almost certainly provoke the Chinese authorities which at that stage sought every opportunity to attack the HK Government. If it did nothing, the Government laid itself open to complaints that it was failing in its duty and creating serious health and other problems liable to spread elsewhere in the territory. It was necessary to move a little bit at a time. Apart from the cleaning efforts of the USD in the Walled City, a fire at one side gave an opportunity for the Government to clear that part, fill it to proper levels, and create a park to provide the proportion of district open space required under town planning guidelines. This nibbling at the edges continued until the whole area was eventually cleared. The revolting image of the Walled City is now no more than a memory, together with archival photographs.

Chapter XXXVIII

Up till the 1970s, most European families in HK employed Chinese servants, often a cookboy and a wash amah, dressed in white Chinese jacket and black trousers. If the family included children, then a baby amah might be employed too. The amahs were often single women, loyal and hardworking, with a rudimentary knowledge of English, but understanding each other was seldom a problem if the employers also spoke a few words of Cantonese. There were standard wages, an extra month's salary as bonus at Chinese New Year, agreed holidays, and a degree of trust. There were of course bad servants and bad employers, but by and large the parties got on well together. The servants lived on the premises in their own rooms, with their own kitchen. When the time for retirement came along, some moved into Buddhist retreats where they could live quietly thereafter amongst contemporaries, either free of charge or for modest amounts provided they had contributed monthly whilst in employment. Otherwise, retiring amahs returned to their families in their native village.

But it could be a lonely life. As the years passed and new ideas spread with the advent of popular magazines, radio and television, an increasing number of amahs started to cut off their customary pigtails and adopt permanent waves or other hairstyles. Young girls were no longer prepared to look for jobs as baby amahs or wash amahs, when they could perhaps earn as much or more working in offices or in industry, living at home, and spending all day amongst other Chinese in more sociable conditions. The supply of amahs and cookboys virtually dried up. They were replaced by the growing influx of Filipina maids who spoke English and were usually efficient and competent. In later days, the Central District on Sundays was a sight to behold, with hundreds of Filipina girls on their weekly holiday sitting and strolling about, eating and drinking, chatting in a twitter of Tagalog.

Chinese families had equally employed cookboys and amahs, and latterly took on Filipina maids. But often part of the household work was undertaken by female relatives (usually unmarried and otherwise largely on their own), who lived free as members of the family in return for their help.

The scarcity of Chinese servants helped in some ways. European housewives who, in the UK or elsewhere had done all the work themselves in the home, found themselves in HK at a loose end in the former prevailing HK culture of servants running the house. There was virtually nothing for them to do but supervise. To fill up their time, some wives took jobs or found openings in working for voluntary organisations. Others stuck to the social round and combed the shops. The new scarcity of staff prompted some wives to go back to their former role of housewives, doing the shopping, cooking and cleaning themselves, with perhaps a weekly visit from one of the new breed of travelling cleaners. For expatriate wives and children from a temperate climate arriving in HK for the first time, the summer temperatures and crowded life could bewilder and dismay them. To help them find their feet, the standard practice was for a senior or middling member of the husband's department or company to advise on what to do, for instance with information about schools, transport, shopping, doctors, sport. It was customary to introduce the newcomer to other people and generally help them along. The pattern was probably the same in all overseas territories.

Chapter XXXIX

Whilst I was Commissioner for Transport (1971-4) in offices on the top floor of the Chater Road multi-storey car park, an issue arose in respect of a branch office in nearby Murray House. Dating from 1846, this building was one of the oldest Colonial-style structures in HK and had originally been an army officers' mess. During the Japanese occupation, it had been the headquarters of the Kempeitai, the Japanese intelligence service which was notorious for the torture and executions carried out there. This wartime activity gave the place an unwelcome flavour. Now, there were reports that Transport staff had seen ghosts on the premises and were reluctant to continue working there. Clearly, immediate action was needed if there was not to be a complete stoppage. Chinese staff take these matters seriously and are far from sceptical about reports of ghosts which tend to be regarded as harmful, or at least frightening, to live people.

I therefore got in touch with the chief abbot of the Buddhist Association, whom I knew slightly, and secured his agreement to carrying out a ceremony of exorcism in a couple of days' time, with no publicity. (I was doubtful whether the Government would be happy with what I was doing.) When I turned up for the ceremony, I was horrified to discover huge crowds surrounding the premises. It was only with difficulty that I managed to get to a position where I could take part in the ceremony (which was televised). The Buddhists had obviously sought maximum publicity. In the event, it caused no harm and the ceremony certainly did for the ghosts which made no further appearance.

But the publicity media made a meal of the event, covering every aspect. Afterwards, I was required to give three TV interviews and five radio interviews, all with the same question: as you are not a Buddhist, why did you take part in a Buddhist ceremony? The answer was simple. If the Transport Department offices should be overrun by rats, I would obviously call in the rat-catchers. In the same manner, if the problem were ghosts, I would call in the ghost-catchers, and if this meant taking part in a Buddhist ceremony, I was happy to do so. But this did not mean that I was a Buddhist. The overriding point was to take steps to ensure that staff of the Transport Department could get back to work without being frightened to death by ghosts.

The ceremony was an interesting exercise that might occur only in the relaxed atmosphere of HK. A West Indian had earlier suggested to me that pepper should be scattered round the area where the ghosts had been seen. Pepper is apparently the standard antidote in the West Indies, but I rejected this not only because it would not help to have staff sneezing their heads off, but more importantly it was not a Chinese remedy and therefore would not be regarded as effective. It was important to employ a traditional local practice that would secure staff confidence.

It so happened that in September 1997 I visited China and enquired to what extent *fung shui* was still followed. The answer was that *fung shui* was a superstition not accepted in China, nor were stories about ghosts and extraterrestrial beings. In other words, the Buddhist ceremony of exorcism in the Transport Department offices could never have happened in China because reports of ghosts could not be accepted. It was hard to believe that China could have wiped out such firmly held beliefs as *fung shui* and ghosts, which now presumably survive only in overseas communities of Chinese outside China. It seems amazing that the former beliefs of hundreds of millions of Chinese could be changed in this manner. But it is always possible that the practice continues amongst older Chinese in a quiet way in odd corners. A comparable example lies in the popular survival of the Orthodox Church in present-day Russia despite its having been banned for seventy years by the previous communist regime.

Chapter XL

In the late 1970s, the Government created the Antiquities Advisory Board (of which I was the first chairman), with responsibility for preserving worthwhile objects from the past. This mainly covered buildings but also included features such as neolithic rock carvings, original milestones, old forts, and suchlike. Dr Solly Bard, the executive secretary and the leading light of the archaeological society, was tireless in seeking out Chinese antiquities in the NT, such as ancestral halls, libraries, temples, clan meeting places, Imperial Chinese forts. A number of rescue operations had to be urgently performed in the face of impending public works. When a contract had been let for the construction of the High Island reservoir in the north-east NT, we got wind of a potential archaeological find in an area about to be developed. I had to persuade a reluctant contractor that we would not hold up his work but would complete the dig in a day or two. The remains of a centuries-old wooden boat and some of its cargo were collected, in a blaze of TV cameras and media photographers. Wearing one of my other hats, a botanical rescue operation was also mounted to collect large quantities of orchids, shrubs, ferns and plants for planting elsewhere before bulldozers and water should obliterate them.

Another rescue operation was carried out on the island of Chek Lap Kok before work started on levelling the island for the present airport. Numerous archaeological artifacts were recovered.

Identifying potential antiquities was fairly straightforward. But problems arose where such buildings were privately owned. In some cases, we were too late. For instance, a rapacious landowner had already demolished a fine stone ornamental gateway. Another allowed the premises to collapse through deliberate neglect. Where this had happened, there was nothing we could do except redouble efforts to get to the others in time. Even there, private owners emphasised their desire to develop the site by knocking down the antiquity and were bought off by an agreed formula to compensate them by allocation elsewhere of a site of equal value for development. Legal protection for these monuments required approval by Executive Council which did not always look favourably on relics of the past and had to be quite properly informed in each case of possible recurrent financial commitments towards future maintenance.

In one way or another, a wide selection of HK's past was saved, structurally preserved, and made available for the public to see and enjoy. Memorial plaques were erected on buildings where famous people had lived or where memorable events had taken place. A series of plaques were mounted in the Central District of HK to mark the successive stages of reclamation. At the top of Duddell Street in Central District, original gas-operated street lights were preserved. In Stanley Military Cemetery, garrison graves from the 1840s are maintained, likewise military graves and monuments in the HK Cemetery in memory of those who died in actions against pirates or otherwise on the China Station.

The neolithic rock carvings are on vertical faces, mostly on outlying islands, with swirling or geometric designs. Their proximity to sea level in some cases may be a matter of their having been cut long before general sea levels rose. Worried that vandals might daub them, a perspex cover was fixed over them, but this was not always helpful, as accumulated salt and dirt tended to prevent seeing through. On the other hand, it did put a stop to vandalism.

The members of the Antiquities Advisory Board were almost all local Chinese, academics or architects with an interest in the subject. Before discussing the merits of any particular case, we always visited at least once, and sought views from those of valued judgment. It was noticeable how antiquities legally declared as monuments and duly publicised drew people's interest. The process was far from being an academic exercise of interest to only a tiny minority. But it did bring out a new feature. As mentioned, some owners in the NT were more concerned with the possible financial return from developing the site of a monument on their land than in preserving the monument. They tended to see preservation and structural maintenance as a continual financial burden with no obvious return. Too often the retort was 'If the Government wants me to keep this structure, then the Government will have to be responsible for its maintenance and I will open a restaurant next door.' Needless to say, the Government was reluctant to enter into any such open-ended commitment. The attitude of such private owners was understandable although unhelpful. In the business world of HK, self-interest and the rice bowl of the family held higher priority than preserving relics of the past.

Passing through a village in the NT, I saw an elderly villager sitting outside the door of his house and playing with a small girl. I pointed to the two parts of a nearby grindstone and asked, 'Does your grand-daughter know what those are?'

'No, of course not. They haven't been used since the end of the War,' was the reply.

'Would you be prepared to give them to the Museum of History so that the public can learn how villagers used to live?'

'Yes, for $10,000.'

Again, it was an attempt to exploit an opportunity for the benefit of the family, coupled with a failure to appreciate how HK had changed in post-war years and the extent of a potential gap in public knowledge of the past.

Chapter XLI

There is little doubt that in its formative post-war years HK has developed its own identity and way of life. Its residents have expectations which it requires its government to meet, not only in the restrained regulation of its business and financial world but also in the field of housing, medical care, education, traffic, recreation and culture. Freedom of expression for both the publicity media and the individual has long been an established feature of the territory. Public scrutiny has kept the civil service on its toes, with timely criticism of any failure to maintain standards, whether in the conduct of the Police, Post Office, or in refuse collection. Left to itself, there is every reason to suppose that HK will manage its own affairs with flair, dedication, and the right degree of sophisticated conservatism.

The miracle of HK is largely a matter of people and their restless push for trade, development and self-expression. It is by no means all a drive for money. The growth of interest in the arts and culture is phenomenal: literature, painting, music, dancing, drama, sport and the environment, in both Chinese and Western fields, are now all highly developed. My impression is that the cry in the latter days of the British administration for democracy was limited to comparatively few individuals and that the vast majority of the population was more concerned that the new regime should not destroy the freedom and loose rein enjoyed under the previous British regime. In its last decade, the former HK Government at all levels had been largely staffed by Chinese under a deliberate policy of preferment over Europeans, as a means of ensuring continuity of standards. When I first joined, my own Administrative Officer grade consisted of about twenty officers occupying top posts, with only one Chinese officer. Today the grade consists of over 400 officers, almost entirely Chinese. The pace of life in

HK is faster than in most other places. Some might call it exhausting. Certainly, compared to the easy quiet life of Western Australia where I now live, visits to HK emphasise the contrast.

And so it was with a feeling of nostalgia but with a sense of the rightfulness of the occasion that my family and I attended the hand-back of HK to China on 1 July 1997. HK is geographically a part of China and its population tends to show its identity with China whilst at the same time wishing to preserve its former way of life.

The British farewell ceremony took place out of doors from 6.15 p.m. to 7.30 p.m. on Monday, 30 June on the former site of the Royal Naval basin of HMS Tamar which had been filled in and tarmac-surfaced. Open stands were erected on both sides, with a covered VIP stand on the third side facing the harbour where the Royal Yacht *Britannia* and HMS *Chatham* were moored alongside. The 14,000 invitees (mostly Chinese) were required to shuffle along outside in a lengthy queue to show tickets, pass through a metal detector arch, collect an umbrella, and make their way to their allotted stand. It had rained on and off for the previous two weeks (the wet season in HK runs from May to September) and the umbrella was needed to keep off the light rain that was then falling. Happily the invitation specified neat casual dress. This was just as well in the hot and humid conditions, and even more welcome with what followed.

As darkness fell, the band and drums of the Royal HK Police Force ('Royal' ceased at midnight when all badges were changed) marched and counter-marched, followed by a massed Bands' performance by musicians from the Royal Marines, Scots Guards and the Highland Bands, together with the pipes and drums of the 1st Bn The Black Watch, and the Brigade of Gurkhas. Three Guards of Honour marched on: one from each Service (the Army one consisted of The Black Watch, the last British regiment to serve in HK). The Prince of Wales, dressed in white Naval tropical uniform, drove up in a Rolls Royce, accompanied by Mr Patten, the 28th and last Governor of HK dressed in a business suit (the Governor's formal summer uniform looks awful). They were greeted with cheers and a General Salute and took their places in the front row of the covered VIP stand (where they were subject to more

Part of the farewell ceremony marking the handback of Hong Kong to China (30/6/97), on a soaking wet night. The RAF contingent is in the foreground, with the Black Watch in kilts in the centre, and the Royal Naval contingent beyond.

rain than in the rows further back). A huge TV screen with its back to the harbour allowed us all to have close-up views of the action in the arena.

In the general open stands, guests huddled under a sea of umbrellas, getting gradually soaked, as much from the rain running off the umbrellas of those in front as from the rain blown slantwise. The more far-sighted had brought plastic bags and newspapers to sit on, but even these precautions were no match for the prevailing damp.

Dancers and schoolchildren provided imaginative tableaux like a mini-opening of the Olympic Games, with music by the HK Philharmonic Orchestra, the HK Chinese Orchestra, and local choirs, performing from stands near the harbour. The pageant continued with the traditional sunset ceremony of lowering the Union Standard and the HK flag. The Governor made a stirring and reflective speech that was greeted with cheers and much foot-stamping in the stands (clapping was minimal as hands were busy holding umbrellas). As Prince Charles stepped forward to make his speech, the heavens opened and the rain poured down. In the open and without an umbrella, he was soon soaked, with the water dripping off his nose. The drumming of the tropical downpour almost drowned the sound of his speech. A Pipe-Major was due to play a lament as a lone floodlit piper in the middle of the darkened arena. But, after fiddling with his sodden pipes, he could produce only a weak watered version that fought a losing battle with the noise of the rain. The unfortunate troops on parade stood their ground, drilled faultlessly and marched off splashing through at least an inch of water on the ground. The high standard of drill was a tribute to the hard work of Garrison Sergeant Major V. Bell, Coldstream Guards.

As the downpour eased to a lighter rain and spectators began to disperse, the more enterprising made a beeline for the cover of the rapidly emptying covered VIP stand, from where they might have a drier view of the coming British fireworks display (the Chinese gave an even bigger display on the following night). The rest of us made do with the middle of the parade ground for the ten minutes or so of non-stop display over the middle of the harbour. Star bursts, fiery rain, and explosions rent the sky as the crowd gave vent to the Cantonese exclamation of 'Wah'. Happy and sodden, the crowd set off for the line of buses drawn up outside, to get ready to watch on TV the final hand-back ceremony at midnight in the Great Hall of the new Convention Centre jutting out into the harbour from HK island.

The British VIPs for the ceremony included Prince Charles, the Prime Minister (Mr Blair), the Foreign Secretary (Mr Cook), Baroness Thatcher, and other distinguished guests too numerous to mention. On the Chinese side were Mr Jiang Zemin (President), Mr Li Peng (Prime Minister) and Mr Tung Chee-hwa (Chief Executive of the SAR). A small three-man British guard of honour (one from each Service) under a Naval officer took up position to one side of the four flag poles, whilst a similar goose-stepping Chinese guard formed up on the other side. Prince Charles and President Jiang made speeches, returned to their seats, looked at each other, and rose simultaneously to meet and shake hands. The Union Standard and former blue HK flag were slowly lowered whilst the Chinese flag and the new SAR flag were at the same time hoisted at the stroke of midnight. After 156 years, HK had now returned to China.

It so happened that, en route to China, I visited HK again for a few days in early September. The place looked the same as it had two months earlier. Friends living there confirmed that there had been no change, and this was emphasised in reported speeches by Mr Tung Chee-hwa (Chief Executive) and Mr Donald Tsang (Financial Secretary; he used to serve in my department years ago). To drive home the point internationally, the annual meeting of heads of the World Bank and the International Monetary Fund was held in HK (and not in Beijing) in late September when Mr Jiang Zemin (President of China), as leader of the host nation, made the point that China had no intention of interfering in the administration of HK. Except for defence and foreign relations, HK could run itself.

There is every reason to suppose therefore that HK can carry on as before, at least for the next fifty years when its status as a Special Administrative Region is due for review. At three of the five airports in China that I passed through in September, strings of bunting with the HK flag were still flying in celebration of the territory's return to China. It looks as if HK has been well supplied with the Chinese medicine for longevity.

Note. The Urban Council was abolished at the end of 1999.

Appenⴂix A

SOME CHINESE CUSTOMS IN THE NEW TERRITORIES

GLOSSARY

1. Succession
2. Adoption
3. *Ching sheung* or *sheung tin* land
4. Land held by clans
5. Family disputes
6. Marriage by proxy
7. *Sam p'o tsai*
8. Customary agricultural leases
9. Graves
10. House-building
11. Some *fung shui* problems
12. Oaths
13. Money loan associations
14. Names

1. SUCCESSION

(a) By Chinese custom there is no such thing as testamentary disposition of property. All a man's will can do is permit his widow(s) to remarry, and to moralise for the sons' edification. It is doubtful whether by English law a NT domiciled person can make a valid will disposing of NT property otherwise than as custom would have directed anyhow. See the Report of the Chinese Law and Custom Committee.

(b) The custom is that land is inherited by all the sons of the deceased, whether by a *kit fat* (結發) or *tin fong* (填房) wife or by a concubine. They all inherit as tenants in common. In some cases, the father of the eldest grandson receives a double or larger share. Since daughters marry and join their husband's family, they do not qualify for inheritance. In some cases the widow or concubine will also inherit, but this is by arrangement among the parties and it is usual for the widow or concubine only to have control over the land in the capacity of manager of a *Tso* (祖). This ensures that the land cannot be disposed of without the consent of the members of the *Tso* (祖).

180

(c) When the sons have married and started families, they may divide the property amongst themselves. Often one share is retained in the name of a *Tso* (祖), so as to provide income for ancestral worship.

(d) Where there are no sons, the property is inherited by the nearest male relative of the deceased. This is often a nephew, brother, uncle or cousin, and excludes all daughters. A son is usually adopted for the purpose of inheritance.

(e) Where there are no children and no close relatives, a widow on occasion may occupy her late husband's property provided there are no family or clan objections, but more often the family will regard the adoption of a son as essential for purposes of inheritance.

(f) Cases have been known where a rich landowner during his lifetime has assigned property into the name of a thrifty concubine. Although under the English law of real property, the concubine would thereby be free to dispose of her property as she pleased, the custom is that she may not alienate the land but may enjoy its benefit only during her lifetime, after which the property reverts to the *Tso* (祖) or main family.

2. ADOPTION

Leaving aside maternal instincts which often lead a childless married woman to adopt a boy or girl, the primary purpose of adoption under Chinese custom is to provide a male for the inheritance of land, and for worshipping the ancestors. It is a business transaction rather than an emotional satisfaction.

(a) Generally, a nephew or clansman of a younger generation is adopted. In many cases, however, the generation of the adopted child is not important. He may even be of the same age as the adoptive parents.

(b) Adoption need not take place during the lifetime of the adoptive parents. One or other of the adoptive parents may have died, and I have met a case where both parents had been dead a year before adoption took place.

(c) Adoption is a formal process that not only requires action on the part of the adoptive parents but also requires the approval of the elders of the family and the clan who normally signify it by attending a feast to eat ceremonial pork. This explains an adoption after the death of the adoptive parents.

(d) The adopted person renounces all rights of succession and inheritance in his natural family. Instead, he acquires these rights in the family by which he has been adopted.

(e) Occasionally, an adopted son attempts to renounce his adoption. I have met one case of this where all parties agreed and which was accordingly approved. Whether the renunciation revests in the son the succession rights in his natural family which he lost by adoption is a difficult question and I think must depend on the particular circumstances of each case.

3. *CHING SHEUNG* (蒸賞) OR *SHEUNG TIN* (賞田) LAND

(a) This is land bequeathed by the original owner or set aside by his inheritors for the specific purpose of ancestral worship. It is usually held in the name of a clan that bears the original owner's name. Rent and proceeds from the land are devoted primarily to the worship of ancestors, and secondarily to the education of members of the clan, relief of poor members, marriage and funeral expenses of members etc.

(b) The land cannot be alienated without the consent of the representatives and elders of the whole clan.

(c) The land is normally cultivated by distribution amongst members of the clan or by lease to a member.

4. LAND HELD BY CLANS

(a) Portions of property owned by a clan (*tso* 祖) are sometimes leased to a family within the clan. These families have often cultivated the same fields for generations, paying an annual rent to the clan accountant. Sub-letting is frowned on and generally forms grounds for cancelling the lease. Alternatively, the various families of a *Tso* (祖) may cultivate the land for a year at a time in rotation and at a fixed annual rent.

(b) Another method of leasing *tso* (祖) property within the clan is to hold an auction where the highest bidder for the annual lease is granted the tenancy for the following year. Money derived from the bid is devoted to ancestral worship etc. as stated in paragraph 3(a) above.

(c) Proper granting of leases by the trustee of the clan is not a regular feature and generally forms a large proportion of land disputes by reason of its omission.

5. FAMILY DISPUTES

The first and most important step is to discover the status of the parties, i.e. are they properly married by Chinese custom or are they cohabiting under some lesser bond?

(a) *Kit fat* (結髮) marriage. This is the traditional form of marriage and assumes that the parties were single and unmarried beforehand. Essential features are exchanges of horoscopes etc. beforehand by the respective families, negotiations by a go-between, signing of the red paper of betrothal, bridal chair (or taxi) from the bride's home to her groom's, feast at groom's house to announce the fact of marriage. It is not usual to omit any of these details, of which the red paper is perhaps the most important. However, there are occasional cases where the red paper is replaced by a certificate signed by both parties and by witnesses to the ceremony.

(b) *Tin Fong* (填房) marriage. Where one of the parties to a *kit fat* marriage dies or is formally divorced, the surviving spouse may subsequently contract another formal marriage which is quite distinct from concubinage. It carries all the force of a *kit fat* marriage.

(c) Concubine. A concubine has a recognised legal status under Chinese custom and should not be regarded as an immoral plaything. Although a rich man, apart from his *kit fat* wife, may take more than one concubine in a fashion that leaves little doubt as to his uxorious mettle, one of the commoner purposes of taking a concubine is to provide the sons that the *kit fat* wife has perhaps failed to produce. The introduction of a concubine into a household is normally a formal process involving due recognition by the family and friends. It is an open matter, like marriage, and implies nothing indiscreet. As far as possible, husbands try to provide separate households for a wife and a concubine who on the whole tend to fight occasionally. Attempts to claim status as a 2nd wife, a level wife (*p'eng tsai* 平妻) or any other variation, should be resisted. Some experts state that by custom a Chinese is monogamous. As a rule he has only one customarily recognised wife or principal spouse, any other women with whom he co-habits being either a concubine (in the Chinese customary sense) or a kept woman.

(d) Kept women, i.e. women who regularly live with a man without being *kit fat* (結髮) or *tin fong* (填房) wives or a concubine, are most frequently met amongst refugees from CT. They differ clearly from concubines in that there is no recognised ceremony for their entry into the household. More often their presence is concealed from the wife, at any rate until the birth of a child. Away from their homes and any social conscience born of fear of ridicule by friends or relatives, refugees tend to form relations with each other on a very temporary basis. They drift together and drift apart without much difficulty.

Having discovered the status of the parties, the dispute can be investigated. As far as possible, it is best to avoid laying blame too heavily on any party since the ultimate object is to persuade them to drop their differences and return home ready to give married life another chance. Too much airing of grievances and bitterness destroys any atmosphere for reconciliation. I often suggest a trial period varying from a week to a month. If, however, things are hopeless, then the only solution is a divorce or separation. A divorce affects only *kit fat* (結髮) and *tin fong* (填房) marriages. Where a woman is a concubine or kept, the parties are free to separate when they please. The divorce or separation of the parties is only the first step. The real trouble comes in dividing up the children and the property. Customarily, sons are returned to the husband, provided he is fit to look after them and maintain them. Daughters remain with the mother. Powers to assist are contained in the Infants Custody Ordinance (Cap. 13) which is not worried about marriage of the parents. Division of property often founders on the question of return by the woman of the clothes and gold ornaments given her as wedding presents by her husband. There is no hard and fast rule in the matter but, in general, where I have thought the woman at fault, I have tried to persuade her to return the presents.

Occasionally a dispute concerns maintenance of the wife by her husband. Provided the parties are properly married, powers are contained in the Separation and Maintenance Orders Ordinance (Cap. 16).

Amongst NT villagers, virginity in brides is highly prized and loss of it before marriage may form grounds for return of a wife to her parents after consummation. In some parts of the interior, it is the custom that only virgins may ride to their future husband's home in a bridal chair. Non-virgins, e.g. widows, are required to advertise the fact by a pedestrian progress under a black umbrella to which is tied a piece of red ribbon.

6. MARRIAGE BY PROXY

(a) Although it is rarely met, there is a form of customary marriage by proxy, which has all the force of, and to all intents and purposes is, a *kit fat* (結髮) marriage. The bride comes to the groom's house and all the ordinary procedure of a wedding is observed, except that the groom is represented by a cockerel. Without being sure, I assume that this custom arose from a regular absence of overseas Chinese from their homes. Certainly, it is the bride who is always present; there is no customary marriage by proxy where the bridegroom is present and the bride absent.

(b) The actual details of the marriage ceremony may be obtained from the SCA where Mr D.R. Holmes compiled an interesting record from a recent case.

7. *SAM P'O TSAI* (新抱仔)

(a) A *sam p'o tsai* (新抱仔) is a young girl who has been reared by a family not her own with the specific object of marrying her to one of the sons of that family. The practice is normally confined to poorer households which fear that, when their children reach marriageable age, the family may not be in a financial position to exchange the necessary gifts for betrothal. Failure to observe tradition in this respect would involve loss of face. A young girl will therefore be handed over to the family of the boy whom she is due to marry. Sometimes the bargain is free, sometimes a token payment is made, sometimes quite a large sum of money changes hands. The money is usually wrapped in red paper to ensure a lucky transaction. There is no fixed age for the entry of the girl into her new home. It may be when she is only a few years old or it may be when she is up to fifteen years old. She becomes, until marriage, just another worker in the household.

(b) The *sam p'o tsai* (新抱仔) is traditionally carried into her new home on the back of a woman, under an open umbrella to which is tied a piece of red cloth. Sometimes, however, an older girl will be transported in a bridal chair. Crackers are fired and there is a sacrifice of chicken and pork to the ancestors, as well as a burning of joss sticks to inform the ancestors of the arrival of the girl into her new family.

(c) At the son's coming of age (between 16 and 18), the couple are ready to be married, provided the girl is sufficiently developed. If not, the ceremony is deferred. The ceremony usually takes place at midnight or in the early hours of the morning in the temple or in the house, with the object of informing the ancestors. Being ancestor worship, which can be performed only by males, the girl remains at home out of the way and no members of her family may be present. A large sieve, usually of bamboo, is placed on the ground. In the centre of it, the bridegroom stands on a rice measure (*tau* 斗), with red cloths draped over his left and right shoulders. He wears a felt hat with silver flowers round it or a feather. In olden times, a Chinese tall hat was worn but, when this fell out of fashion, the felt hat was adopted as the most respectable of modern headgear. The feather represented the old Imperial custom of presenting a feather to the best scholars.

(d) Shortly after this ceremony, and on the same day, comes the actual wedding, which is known as the crowning, when relatives and friends of both families are invited. Relations are given cups of tea by the bridal couple. The important feature is that the marriage dates from this ceremony, not from the time of entry of the *sam p'o tsai* into her new family, although a girl will sometimes say that she was married, for instance, at the age of six.

(e) There is no traditional requirement for the *sam p'o tsai* to marry the son. I have met several cases where the girl declined marriage and the parties agreed to separate. Brought up in a brother and sister atmosphere, the boy and girl may lack the right approach to marriage.

8. CUSTOMARY AGRICULTURAL LEASES

(a) In the absence of a written agreement to the contrary, leases of agricultural land are normally on an annual basis. Payment of rent may be in cash or in 'kuk' (穀) either in one lump sum or after each of the two rice harvests. Most leases are verbal.

(b) It is common practice for members of the lessee's family to take over his lease in the event of his death. Acceptance of rent by the lessor in these cases implies recognition of the new lessee.

(c) Sub-letting is a practice more common amongst immigrant vegetable farmers than paddi farmers. It is rare to find an original lease that prohibits sub-letting and in general landowners do not seem to object to it as long as their rents come in. In some cases, they even collect rent direct from the sub-lessee.

(d) It is customary for a landlord to reduce the fixed rent in respect of a harvest which has been particularly poor, but discretion is entirely in the hands of the landlord and request must be made by the tenant himself before the crop is actually harvested, so that the landlord may have a chance of examining the crop to check the truth of the claim.

(e) The termination of an annual lease of paddi land is affected customarily by the landowner giving notice, either verbal or written, to the tenant between the time of collecting rent after the second harvest (October/November) and the Winter Solstice (December). The land should then be handed back by the tenant to the landlord at the end of the first moon of the following year, in the case of paddi land.

(f) Leases of vegetable land are customarily for a period of twelve months from the beginning of the 1st moon to the end of the twelfth moon. No set period of notice is required for recovery of the land, but in general the landlord should give sufficient notice to ensure that the tenant does not plant further crops which would carry him beyond the end of the year. Two to three months' notice is probably adequate. Less notice would not be wrong but it might be unreasonable unless the landlord either gave compensation for standing crops or allowed an extension of the lease until the crop was harvested.

(g) Payment of rent for vegetable land is usually in cash in lieu of paddi. Traditionally, paddi land was regarded as more valuable than vegetable land. Since 1950, a reversal in values has taken place and the lack of clear-cut custom regarding vegetable land often gives rise to difficulties.

(h) In the past, recovery of land by a landlord was an unusual occurrence and tenancies often continued for several generations. With the general increase of agricultural activity since 1949 (due to the influx of industrious refugees), tenancies are more frequently called in. Sometimes a mere pretext covers the real reason that a hardworking tenant has spent much capital in improving poor land which the landlord now wishes to lease again at a higher rent. It is always wise before intervening in tenancy cases to be sure that a good reason exists for recovery of the land. These reasons might be that the tenant is a poor one who makes little use of the land; the tenant has failed to pay rent or has otherwise committed a breach of conditions, e.g. illegal temporary structures; the landowner is short of land and has a large family. Where is is necessary on the facts to find in favour of the landlord, it is often easier to persuade the tenant to comply by offering to find him alternative Crown Land.

(i) It is a recurring feature in many cases that tenants tend to sink capital into land, particularly with chicken farms, without having any real lease to protect them. Rapacious landlords take advantage of this and often deliberately refuse to issue written leases. I have had no success whatsoever in trying to educate tenants in this respect.

9. GRAVES

(a) Bodies are normally buried in an earth grave (*huet chong* 血葬) for five years or so. At the end of that time, they are usually exhumed and the bones arranged in an earthenware funerary pot (*kam tap* 金塔). Richer families and clans will sometimes install the exhumed bones in a masonry grave (*shan fan* 山墳) instead of a funerary pot.

(b) *Huet chong* (血葬) and *kam taps* (金塔) are always sited in groups on hillsides or ground where the *fung shui* is good. It is not usual to build or cultivate near these areas.

(c) The choice of site of a *shan fan* (山墳) is again dictated by *fung shui* (風水). Considerable sums of money may be spent in fees for the *fung shui sin shang* (風水先生) and in construction, although workmanship is rarely first class. The site is usually high up, commanding a view of water in some form or other, and on a ridge or spur which represents, for instance, a dragon, snake, shrimp or crab in its formation. The principle is that the animal represented is a beneficial one which will guard the deceased who, in his turn, will watch over the interests of his descendants on this earth if sufficiently propitiated in the next world by his earthly descendants. This conception is important because it explains the strenuous objections usually met where the *fung shui* (風水) of a burial place is disturbed. The commonest objections are against the cutting or digging of the ridge or spur at any point directly above the grave itself, since this will destroy the creature whose influence is protecting the deceased.

(d) Important graves are frequently ones of recorded ancestors or founders of a clan. These graves are normally flanked by two small shrines (*hau to* 后土), one on either side at a distance of roughly twenty feet, and sometimes one above as well. Their object is to persuade the earth god to look after the grave.

(e) A *shan fan* sometimes falls into disuse and neglect by reason of the disappearance of all descendants or through other reasons. A sure sign of this is the removal of the *pei shek* (碑石) or stone plaque on which details of the deceased are recorded. At the two grave-worshipping festivals of Ching Ming (清明) and Chung Yeung (重陽) it is normal to tidy up *huet chong* (血葬), *kam tap* (金塔), and *shan fan* (山墳) and to decorate them with patches of white lime and lucky money as well as joss sticks.

(f) Standing with one's back to the *pei shek* (碑石) of a *shan fan* (山墳) and facing the same way as the grave, a half circle in front with a radius of 10 yards is normally sacrosanct. Disturbance of the ground is regarded with strong disfavour. Traditionally, the left arm of this half moon is protected by a green dragon and the right arm by a white tiger.

189

(g) The degree of *fung shui* (風水) involved is relative and, in some cases where there apparently exists no strong feeling on the subject, a road or cutting may be allowed right up against a grave. At other times, very strong objections indeed may be raised. Generally the strongest feelings lie with clans that have sufficient land and money to carry on traditional ancestor worship and to keep the proper spirit alive.

(h) Ancestral graves are not necessarily in the same vicinity as the village where the descendants live. Sometimes they are far apart. For instance, the large *Man* (文) clan of *San Tin* (新田) has graves at *Tsuen Wan* (荃灣) and Castle Peak which are visited at the two festivals by a lengthy motorcade of lorries containing worshippers, a band, and enormous quantities of food and drink. This separation of distance represents only the dictates of good *fung shui* (風水) and does not mean that the clan has shifted its village at some past stage in history.

10. HOUSE-BUILDING

(a) It often occurs that an owner of building land or of agricultural land to be converted to building status applies for leave to start building at once without waiting for the completion of normalities, e.g. scrutiny of plans, signature of papers, etc. His grounds for wishing to cut procedure short are that a lucky day for building is approaching and that he cannot afford to miss the opportunity. Attempts of this sort, however importunate, can usually be resisted by instructing the applicant to continue with house-building ceremonies without actually doing any building itself.

(b) The ceremonies themselves are of three separate types and need not necessarily take place in any particular order or on the same day. There may be a different lucky day for each. They are equally practised amongst Cantonese and *Hakka* (客家). Their expenses, particularly of entertainment, are such that they form a large part of building costs and to some extent must be reckoned as a deterrent to permanent buildings, at any rate amongst the poorer villagers.

(c) The lucky day is chosen by the geomancer comparing the applicant's time and date of birth against the Chinese almanac which records which days are luckiest for performing certain things. As this method of selection is employed in various other domestic circumstances, e.g. marriage, opening a business etc., a record of a child's name and date of birth is of particular importance for its future prosperity.

(d) *On mun* (安門) consists of setting up the front door on the building site itself. Three lengths of bamboo, to which is attached a piece of red paper with the characters (安門大吉), are erected in the shape of a doorway, i.e. two uprights and one crosspiece. No feast or celebration is required.

(e) *Sheung leung* (上梁) is the more important ceremony and involves the erection of the main ridge-pole of the roof. Several days before the actual ceremony, two unpainted wooden uprights are set up on the building site. On the lucky day chosen, a red painted beam which is traditionally of China fir is placed between two tables or stools. The applicant and his family will worship the centre of the beam, praying for prosperity within the new house. The youths of the village, most of whom will already be assembled, are then invited to hoist the beam up to the two uprights and to lash it on. Meanwhile, drums and gongs will be beaten. When the beam is erected, red string will be used to attach the following to it: a piece of red cloth; some small taros (a big taro has many small ones round it, symbolising a mother with many children); two small bags of red cloth, one containing *kuk* (穀) and the other *mai* (米) (representing riches in much rice); a red bamboo sieve (the numerous holes represent mouths of a large family); two bundles of red chopsticks (the Cantonese *faai chi* (筷子) for chopsticks is punned into *faai chi* (筷子), meaning quick sons); several onions (Cantonese *chung* 葱 is punned into *chung meng* (聰明), meaning clever); several garlic bulbs (Cantonese *suen tau* (蒜頭) is punned into (算), meaning ingenious); one pair of black trousers (Cantonese *foo* (褲) is punned into *foo kwai* (富貴), meaning rich); two paper lanterns (Cantonese *tang* 燈 is punned into *tim ting* (添丁), meaning getting a son). A feast is then held, to which the applicant invites clansmen, friends and relatives, and specially baked cakes are distributed to children. In due course, the remainder of the house is built round the beam. The various articles attached to it are left hanging, except that for some reason the pair of black trousers are usually detached.

(f) *Tin Kei* (奠基) represents digging the foundations. A small channel is first dug to one side of the building site and a number of stones or bricks are placed on top of each other inside the channel.

(g) When the house is completed, a form of house-warming is held. Two red-painted rice measures (*tau* 斗) are filled, one with *kuk* (穀) and the other with *mai* (米), and candles and joss-sticks placed standing in the rice. Worshipping takes place at the shrines of the earth god *t'o tei* (土地) and kitchen god within the house. If the applicant can still afford it, he holds a feast for friends and relatives who often bring presents of mirrors and furniture.

11. SOME *FUNG SHUI* (風水) PROBLEMS

(a) Certain localities, particularly hills, are sometimes regarded as throwing out good or bad influences, according to the animal which the locality represents. In the same manner, strong objections are frequently raised to the opening of windows in a house that faces some other house or temple. The window represents the open mouth of a tiger ready to swallow up the occupants of the building facing it. A lamp flashing in the direction of a house is equally obnoxious.

(b) Antidotes to these evil rays or influences are often difficult to apply. One method is for the aggrieved householder to put up a *paat kwa* (八卦) or eight-sided diagram on the outside of their house. Alternatively, a mirror sometimes will suffice to reflect the evil rays. A third method is to erect some effective barrier in between, such as trees or bamboos, with a temporary wall until the trees have attained sufficient height and bushiness to be an effective screen.

(c) These objections are for the most part confined to Cantonese rather than *Hakka* (客家). However, because of their greater belief in animism, *Hakka* (客家) are the more concerned with *fung shui* (風水), trees and rocks, damage to which they will strenuously oppose.

12. OATHS

(a) Before the lease of the NT to the Crown in 1898 and the coming of

British law, the question of which party to a dispute was telling the truth was customarily settled by a form of trial by ordeal in a temple. Both parties would attend at a mutually agreed temply (*miu* 廟, never a clan temple or *Tsz t'ong* 祠堂) with witnesses and all interested villagers. Each party would then pray to the temple god affirming the truth of his statements in the dispute and inviting the god to do the supplicant an injury if he were not in fact telling the truth. Each party in turn would then attempt to strike off the head of a live cock (colour unimportant) with a single stroke of a chopper. If the head were severed cleanly, the party thereby proved his case. An incomplete severance would show the hollowness of the party's statements, probably because guilty knowledge caused his hand to shake.

(b) In practice, it was seldom that both parties were required to chop off the cock's head. Usually the guilty party would feel himself unable to invite the god's wrath in the preliminary worshipping and would back out. This implied a perhaps greater belief in the omnipotence of the gods than is apparent nowadays when the modern age and Christianity have taken some of the edge off ancient traditions.

(c) The custom is now quite rare, although a case occurred in Tai Po (大埔) in 1948, under the auspices of the then District Officer. Present statutory penalties for breach of oath in judicial proceedings and statutory declarations have almost wholly replaced this custom.

13. MONEY LOAN ASSOCIATIONS

(a) Debt disputes frequently arise as a result of money loan associations. Without a clear idea of their workings, it is impossible to understand the inevitable ramifications of each case.

(b) Such associations are normally formed by groups of persons in close daily contact with each other so as to create mutual trust and confidence. Examples are employees or *fokis* of a shop or even government servants in the same office. The object of the association is to pool the financial resources of the members, with the gambling prospect of each member at some stage being able to use these resources for his own benefit. Each member will eventually get back roughly the same amount of money as he put into the association.

193

(c) There are of course variations but generally the procedure is for a number of persons to club together for a set period which corresponds to the number of persons (e.g. ten persons for ten months). The period can begin at any time and regular meetings are held throughout. In the commonest form of the association, each member will at the first meeting pay to the chairman, who is usually the instigator of the scheme, an agreed sum of money, for example $50.

At the second meeting, all members will in secret tender to the chairman on slips of paper the amount of interest which they are prepared to offer on each member's share. The member who tenders the highest interest, say $5 on $50 shares, is awarded all the members' shares for that meeting. The members are then required to pay over their share ($50) less the highest amount of interest tendered, i.e. $50 less $5 = $45. The winner therefore collects $45 from each member for that meeting. When a member has secured the highest tender, he is thereafter regarded as a dead member and at all further meetings has to pay the full share to the successful tenderer whilst himself being debarred from tendering again. In this manner, each member in turn will eventually at some stage become a successful tenderer. At the last meeting, the one remaining member will collect his full amount back again and he will have profited by the interest accruing on the sums loaned to each successful tenderer during the set period.

(d) In the above form of the association, the chairman collects the fixed sum in full from each member at the first meeting repaying the same amount at each subsequent meeting to the successful tenderer. He gets in effect an interest-free loan. In a different form, the chairman may be in the nature of a professional, charging the successful tenderer each month a commission usually fixed at 50 per cent of the fixed sum. This type of chairman is really acting as a sort of paid manager.

(e) In any form of association, the chairman gives each member at or before the first meeting a booklet containing the names of members and simple rules, including a liability on the chairman in the event of a member dying or backing out.

(f) The aim as far as possible is that each member should at some stage during the set period have the use of the combined shares of all the members. In effect, he is borrowing money at a low rate of interest without knowing exactly when the loan will come. It is the appeal of this gambling element which makes these associations so popular amongst wage-earning Chinese.

(g) The drawbacks are numerous. It is preferable that each member should appear at each meeting if he is not to be deprived of his chances. No member can back out of the association until the full period has elapsed, since otherwise the sum won by the successful tender will be depleted. Most disputes arise by reason of a successful tenderer attempting to back out at an early stage, having obtained a sum of money by means which are hard to define as either larceny, false pretences or embezzlement.

14. NAMES

(a) Throughout his life, a Chinese will often use a bewildering series of names or aliases, each of which usually denotes some stage in life. The practice between men and women is slightly different.

(b) When a child is born, he or she is given a milk name (乳名), chosen well before the full moon feast which normally takes place when the child is a month old. This milk name is used by the child's family and relatives.

(c) At the full moon feast, the parents choose a proper name for the child and then worship the gods (Goddess of Mercy – *Kwun Yam* 觀音; Queen of Heaven – *Tin Hau* 天后; *Kwan Tai* 關帝, etc.) who are informed of the name and asked to give their blessing to its holder.

(d) When the child first goes to school, he or she is traditionally required to kneel before the teacher who invokes the aid of Confucius in assisting the child in studying knowledge and who gives the child a school name (書名). This school name is used by pupils and teacher in school but at home does not normally displace the milk name which the family will continue to use.

(e) On marriage, a man will give up his milk name and will be given an adult name (字名) by his fellow clansmen. Usually the second name will be that of the second name of the clan, e.g. TANG Ping Cheung (鄭炳章) after the TANG Ping Hak Tso (鄭炳克祖).

(f) Finally, in entering business or commerce, a man will frequently assume yet another name, *'pit tsz'* (別字), for purposes of business only.

(g) Apart from the milk name, proper name and school name, a girl will at marriage assume her husband's clan name in front of her own, e.g. HO Fung Ling (何鳳玲), on marrying TANG Man Lin (鄭萬連), becomes TANG HO Fung Ling (鄭何鳳玲).

(h) The reluctance of married women to reveal their full maiden name often leads them to leave off their final name and instead to add the suffix *'shi'* (氏).

Appendix B

CHINESE BURIAL CUSTOMS IN HONG KONG*

Before 1949, burial customs in China were largely geared to the traditions of a predominantly agricultural country. Except in the New Territories, however, Hong Kong was not in a position to follow the same rural traditions of burial procedure and therefore was forced to evolve a pattern more or less of its own. The post-war change of government in China has led to even further changes in local burial customs.

For non-Christian Chinese in Hong Kong, the focus of burial practices is the veneration of family ancestors. In its extreme form this can be taken to mean the belief that, if surviving relatives and descendants pay sufficient respect to their dead, the dead in their turn will exercise a benevolent influence over the lives and prosperity of their family.

The deceased is considered to be in a better position to watch over his earthly descendants if buried close to his native place, where it is also, of course, easier for his family to pay their respects to him. This has led to the practice of conveying the deceased back to the place in China whence he came and interring him in a traditional burial ground. It is well known that, no matter where they die, the bodies of overseas Chinese have, where possible, usually been conveyed back to their homes for burial; when they could afford to do so, relatives have followed this same principle where death occurred in Hong Kong.

---

*The writer wishes to make it clear that, in putting forward this article, he has simply recorded information which has come to his notice incidentally in connection with other duties. He is neither an anthropologist nor a trained research worker, but simply an amateur with an interest.

Coffins and remains of Chinese who died in various parts of the world, e.g. Borneo, the Philippines, Indonesia, the USA, have been shipped to China via Hong Kong which in pre-war and immediately post-war days enjoyed a certain pre-eminence as a transit centre for the onward movement of human remains.

The trans-shipment was not always immediate. Circumstances often imposed some delay. To meet the difficulties of holding the coffin temporarily, the Tung Wah Group of Hospitals in pre-war days set up in Hong Kong a coffin repository in Sandy Bay where remains could be stored on payment of a monthly fee. This repository served its original purpose well till 1949 when difficulties arose in the way of transferring bodies into China. At present, there is virtually no movement of coffins into China, with the result that the repository has gradually accumulated nearly 10,000 coffins, urns and containers. The accommodation ranges from single rooms, where one or more coffins rest on trestles, to larger rooms holding hundreds of coffins, together with exhumed remains in a variety of receptacles, e.g. earthenware urns, rattan baskets, wooden boxes and even second-hand tin containers. In some cases, all trace of the relatives of the deceased has been lost and it is proposed to re-inter such remains in a special Tung Wah plot at the Sandy Ridge Cemetery, to which further reference will presently be made.

A clear pattern is now emerging, whereby Hong Kong has almost ceased to be a transit centre for the conveyance of deceased Chinese to their native place. The next best alternative, both for overseas dead and Chinese residents of Hong Kong itself, is to bury them in Hong Kong instead, though that is not to imply that local cemeteries are doing a brisk business in snapping up overseas trade.

In examining the details of current burial procedure, a distinction must be drawn between the urban areas and the New Territories. In the congested urban areas, where land is needed for development and health measures assume greater importance, there is not the same freedom in choice of burial grounds. Relatives must decide whether to bury the dead in a private cemetery, with higher fees, or in a public cemetery, with lower fees and compulsory exhumation of remains after a period of years.

Taking the urban areas first, let us trace the events of a typical funeral. Unlike the earlier traditional habits of mainland China, where preparations for burial were largely carried out by members of the family, the current practice in Hong Kong is for the relatives, on death occurring in their midst, at once to call in an undertaker or someone from a funeral parlour. The undertaker provides a coffin, encoffins the body and conveys it thus to a cemetery for burial, but he is debarred by law from bringing dead bodies on to his own business premises. A funeral parlour on the other hand has wider scope. Its staff will enter the home of the deceased and remove the body to the parlour, either in a basket-woven container coloured silver, blue or yellow, or on a plain canvas stretcher. The advantage of using a funeral parlour instead of an undertaker lies in the fact that, with the body actually held temporarily on the premises of the parlour, it is possible there to carry out funeral rites which would be otherwise inconvenient where an undertaker conveyed the encoffined body direct from the home to the cemetery.

Chinese in Hong Kong dislike holding a dead body overnight in the private home. They much prefer its immediate removal after death. Neighbours too are far from happy at the thought of death in the near vicinity, nor in earlier days used they to be in favour of allowing the body to be removed in a coffin past their particular floor in a two- or three-storeyed tenement building. Chinese coffins usually consist lengthwise of four sections of tree trunk and are therefore bulky, irrespective of whether the coffin is cheap or one of the expensive polished varieties. Manoeuvring these coffins up and down narrow tenement staircases, with inevitable banging against walls, might be likened to death tapping at the door: a harbinger of bad luck.

To meet this problem of removal from upper floors in the urban areas, it used to be the custom up till five or six years ago to construct a bamboo staging outside the building, so that the coffin could be taken out of the window and be brought down the staging to the hearse in the roadway. The custom has now almost entirely disappeared for a number of reasons, largely economic: new buildings have grown too high for stagings to reach most upper storeys; the cost of long bamboo from China has risen enormously as a result of its use for scaffolding in the current building boom; the practice of glassing-in verandahs and balconies has made windows too small for coffins to fit through; traffic congestion in the streets makes the authorities chary of allowing even more obstruction in the form of these stagings on roads and pavements. To take their place as a means of removing the body from the private premises, basket-woven containers or stretchers have come to be used, and they are far less expensive.

If an undertaker is engaged, he will prepare the body in the deceased's home, encoffin and remove it either direct to the cemetery or to a government cemetery depot in Hong Kong or Kowloon, where it can be held overnight pending government conveyance to a public cemetery. A farewell pavilion at each depot provides free facilities for the relatives to hold services of any denomination or to perform other last rites.

If a funeral parlour is engaged, the body is conveyed in the basket-woven container or stretcher to the parlour for preparation, encoffining and almost invariably a service. In a few cases, embalming is carried out but this is a refinement that seems to hold no particular significance since burial takes place normally within the forty-eight hours allowed by law for the body to remain on the premises. In parts of China, it apparently used to be the custom to delay burial for periods of up to seven weeks. But the more tropical climate of Hong Kong and the ever-present risk of disease have made it necessary to insist on a forty-eight hours limit in funeral parlours.

When encoffined in a funeral parlour, the body is placed in a farewell room where it is customary for the immediate relatives to maintain a vigil (overnight, if necessary) until the time comes for conveyance to a cemetery or crematorium. During the vigil and funeral, the close relatives (i.e. widow and widower, sons and daughters, daughters-in-law and grandchildren) are often dressed in the traditional mourning colour of white, usually in a costume provided by the funeral parlour and consisting, for women, of a white skirt and an upper garment resembling half a sack with one corner placed over the head. Men tend to wear white gowns, with a white band tied round the forehead. A thin surcoat of sackcloth (*haaù ma pò* 孝麻布) may be worn over the white mourning clothes by a widow, daughter and daughter-in-law of the deceased; a son may wear a smaller square of sackcloth over his head.

Friends and relatives will pay their respects to the deceased by bowing towards the coffin three times and once towards the chief mourners, who are usually ranged to one side and may be kneeling with their heads towards the ground. For this public lying in state, the deceased is sometimes placed in a special coffin that leaves the upper portion of the body temporarily exposed. Before burial, the missing portion of the coffin lid will be replaced. The farewell room throughout the vigil and lying in state may be lit with candles and incense sticks, often making the atmosphere uncomfortably heavy and oppressive. In the past, it was customary to bang gongs throughout the vigil, to keep away evil spirits, but this practice is now prohibited to avoid nuisance to neighbours. It is also customary amongst the less well-to-do for the female relatives of the deceased, particularly a widow, to give a public demonstration of grief in the form of wailing, weeping and loud cries. Mute grief would neither satisfy custom nor perhaps offer adequate incentive to the spirit of the deceased to exercise a benevolent influence on his descendants.

In practice, the last rites at a funeral parlour usually continue till midday, for the practical reason that it may take the whole morning to complete formalities such as registering the death and making arrangements with the relevant authorities for burial or cremation. The body is then taken by motor hearse to the cemetery or crematorium, accompanied by relatives. Friends may also accompany the hearse if they wish, but there is no objection to their departing earlier after the last rites have been performed. For a particularly large funeral, the journey to the cemetery may be preceded by a ceremonial procession in the neighbourhood, with funeral bands, mourners on foot, the hearse with the coffin, and large wicker framework plaques covered in silver and blue paper describing the deceased. The writer once saw a one-quarter mile procession, with no less than sixteen separate bands, complete an entire circuit of the Happy Valley racecourse before departing for the cemetery. Some of the funeral bands may be hired by the descendants of the deceased; other bands may be hired by friends wishing to offer condolences.

At the cemetery, the coffin is normally lowered into the grave without further ceremony and the hole filled. Just before the hole is filled, it is customary for each member of the family present to throw in a handful of earth. After filling, two candles are usually lit and placed near the head of the grave and three incense-sticks nearer the foot. Sometimes, absent members of the family may depute other relatives to set out candles and incense-sticks on their behalf, in which case the proportions are still observed. An offering of oranges may be peeled and placed on the grave, together with paper money. Finally, crackers are let off.

Occasionally, after the coffin has been lowered and before the earth is thrown in, a male descendant present will make a cut in a live cock so that blood flows out. The cock will then be held over the grave to allow its blood to drop on the coffin and sides of the hole, in the traditional hope that the breeding properties of the cock will be transmitted to the deceased. Provided that the deceased is over middle age, sex normally makes no difference. A more modern version of this practice omits the incision on the cock, which is simply swung over the hole on the end of a piece of string.

The last rites sometimes involve the assistance of Taoist or Buddhist monks, even though neither the relatives nor the deceased may necessarily profess complete belief in either of those religions. The monks normally appear in a team of five, the leader with the other four ranged in pairs. Their form of service usually follows the pattern of Taoist and Buddhist chanting, accompanied by music, the striking of bells, small brass ringing bowls and wooden sound-boxes (*muk ue* 木魚). In major funerals, where the body is held elsewhere than in a funeral parlour, the last rites may continue for seven full days before burial, with further services every seventh day for a total of forty-nine days. If expense proves too much, some of the weekly services may be omitted but it is customary to include the fifth one, when married daughters and granddaughters are expected to contribute either wholly or in part; the final service is also required. At these weekly rites, the next-of-kin may sometimes cook rice and beans (red and green) which are then eaten by relatives in the hope of attaining long life (*chué shaû faân* 煮壽飯).

Another custom still often encountered is the placing of several pairs of trousers on the deceased, whether male or female. Half a dozen pairs of trousers is not uncommon. Based on a pun between the Cantonese *foò* (褲 trousers) and *foǒ* (富 riches), the object is to provide wealth for the spirit of the deceased. Including jacket and underwear, an even number of garments is normally placed on a male; an odd number on a female.

In the New Territories, there are at present no funeral parlours and few undertakers. As in the agricultural interior of China, practical responsibility still falls mainly on the kinsmen of the deceased. The customary burial of villagers is in two stages: initial coffin burial, and subsequent exhumation and re-interment of remains. Having encoffined the body, the relatives normally sustain the vigil directly outside the home under a temporary shelter. Burial then takes place in a traditional village area, but no monument is erected beyond a small unshaped stone at the head of the grave. After five years or more, the body is exhumed. The bones will be cleaned by the family and be placed either in a funerary urn (*kam t'aàp* 金塔) or in a formal masonry grave (*shaan fan* 山墳) shaped like a horseshoe. In the funerary urn, the bones will be arranged in a manner as if the deceased were sitting in the Buddhist lotus posture.

The siting of the funerary urns and horseshoe graves is of particular importance. Relatives will go to great lengths to ensure that the *fung shui* (風水) of the site is propitious. In other words, they wish to ensure that the benevolent influence of the site will protect the deceased, as a member of the family, so that he in turn will look kindly upon his relatives. The site is usually high up, commanding a view of water and on a ridge or spur which represents, for instance, a dragon, snake, shrimp or crab in its formation. Standing with one's back to a horseshoe grave, one sees a half circle within a radius of ten yards, which is normally regarded as sacrosanct. Disturbance of the ground is regarded with strong disfavour. Traditionally, the left arm of the panorama in front should consist of a long ridge (containing a 'green dragon') and the right arm of a shorter ridge (containing a 'white tiger'). In a horseshoe grave, the exhumed remains are buried in a jar in the centre, just in front of a stone plaque (*pei shêk* 碑石) that records the name of the deceased, the date of his death, and other details. Important graves of recorded ancestors or founders of a clan are often flanked by a small shrine (*haû t'ó* 后土) on either side and sometimes another behind, at a distance of ten to twenty feet from the main grave. The object of the shrines is to persuade the earth god to look after the grave.

Whether the exhumed remains are to be placed in a funerary urn or in a horseshoe grave seems to be governed by the sex and general standing of the deceased in the clan, or even by the financial state of the relatives at the time of exhumation. The remains are normally fit for exhumation after a minimum of five years of burial, but, even so, exhumation should not strictly take place unless there has been no pregnancy amongst the deceased's close female relatives in the immediately preceding nine months. This requirement, which would tend to impose some hardship on the male relatives, can be got round by omitting pregnant wives from the ceremony. There is a belief that exhumation should not take place during the years on which fall the 51st, 61st, 71st and other such birthdays of the male head of the family.

In Chinese public cemeteries, the same principle of exhumation is practised. At the end of each year, the particular coffin section where burials have been taking place is closed and left untouched for five years. At the end of that time, an official notice of intention to clear graves is published, giving relatives six months in which to exhume remains privately and re-inter them in the urn section. Any remains not exhumed privately on the expiry of the period of notice are then exhumed by Government and the remains re-interred in an urn section. The cleared coffin section is then eventually used again for coffin burials.

Applying equally to urban and New Territories burials are the two important grave worshipping festivals of Ching Ming (105 days after the winter solstice, i.e. either 5 or 6 April) and Chung Yeung (9th day of the 9th moon, i.e. in October). The first is the more important. The second was originally not a grave-worshipping festival at all, but an occasion for climbing to the top of a mountain to avoid evil spirits. Since so many graves are situated on hills, the practice of combining the hill climb with an opportunity of worshipping at graves has been developed.

Strict Cantonese belief also requires that, at *ch'un she* (春社), which falls annually about two weeks before the Ching Ming festival, relatives should pay their·respects to persons who have died within the past year. This ceremony usually takes place at home and its participants are restricted to older persons.

At the Ching Ming and Chung Yeung festivals, it is customary for whole families to make an outing to their relatives' graves. There, offerings of pork, fruit and flowers are presented; incense and candles burnt; prayers offered; crackers let off. Minor repairs to the graves may be carried out and undergrowth cut back. Coffin graves in the New Territories may be marked with lime at the end and all types of graves usually have a piece of red paper and another piece of white paper underneath the red, tucked under a stone beside them. Exhumations will often be carried out at the Ching Ming festival. At the Tung Wah coffin repository, caskets of remains are opened and the bones spread out to air on sheets of paper.

Chinese believe that the spirit of a person leaves the body on death. In Hong Kong the general belief is that it descends into hell where the judge decides on the basis of the earthly merits of the deceased whether it may be allowed to return to earth by reincarnation as a child or, if very evil, as an animal. The main fear of the dead consists rather of the belief that to touch the dead is to run the risk of becoming infected by an aura of ill-luck (*sz yan fung* 死人風) whereby all the misfortunes of the deceased will be transmitted.

Amongst fishermen fear of the dead and of ill-luck is particularly pronounced. At Tai O on the north-western end of Lantau, fisherfolk on their deathbed may be taken from their boats to die in a special house maintained for the purpose near the cemetery.

During funeral processions in both the urban areas and the New

Territories, it is the practice to scatter different types of paper, representing money, along the route to the burial ground, particularly at crossroads where traditionally malevolent spirits tend to congregate. It is hoped that in the confusion caused by the evil spirits grabbing the money the spirit of the deceased will be able to pass unscathed. The remainder of the paper money thrown out at points other than crossroads is for the use of the spirit of the deceased in making his way back to his home three days after the death (*saam ch'iu ooi wan* 三朝回魂). In many homes, a corner in a hall or passage may be reserved for a tablet and memorial, to house the spirit on its return to the home. This return of the spirit may at first sight be difficult to reconcile with the belief that the spirit descends into hell. The answer is that according to Chinese belief each dead person has a number of spirits. The descent of one of these spirits into hell is often assisted at the burial by the scattering and burning of specially printed hell bank notes (*meng t'ung chí paî* 冥通紙幣), together with paper effigies of clothes, suitcases, motor cars, steamships, aeroplanes etc., often of most elaborate and detailed construction.

The impact of crowded living conditions, economy and improved public health have had their gradual effect in changing the pattern of Hong Kong burial custom. Except for paupers, by far the greater proportion of Chinese dead from the urban areas (numbering some 10,000) are now buried in the public cemetery at Wo Hop Shek, near Fan Ling in the New Territories. Coffins may be conveyed by rail from Kowloon daily as a service included within the burial fees that are $5 or $15 according to size of coffin. Only some 20 per cent of the coffins are carried to the cemetery by private hearses at the expense of the relatives. Of the balance brought by rail, not more than half are attended by relatives. It is obviously not possible in a public cemetery to site graves in accordance with individual interpretations of *fung shui*. The fact that each coffin is simply allotted the next vacant space in the burial terrace is readily accepted, although it must be admitted that the majority of terraces are well up the hillside with a commanding view of distance and water. Similarly, when the routine six months' notice of intention to exhume remains from the coffin section is given, it is

206

unusual for relatives to clear the graves privately in more than half the cases. The balance is left to Government to clear. The deduction might be drawn that, although there may well be relatives still at hand in Hong Kong, they accept the government service in clearance as perfectly adequate for the purpose and as a useful means of saving themselves expense.

Every year, in addition to Chinese dead mentioned above, the bodies of nearly 10,000 paupers are left to Government to dispose of. The term 'pauper' does not imply that the deceased were homeless and abandoned. Most of the deaths occur in charitable institutes and hospitals. In most cases, there were relatives available but for one reason or another, usually economic, they preferred not to claim the body, being satisfied that the free burial (at the Sandy Ridge Cemetery, Lo Wu) and subsequent exhumation provided by Government would be sufficient to meet changed conditions.

Where possible, attempts are made at public Chinese cemeteries to meet burial customs. Facilities are provided at the Ching Ming and Chung Yeung festivals, in the form of special trains with reduced fares for relatives; crowd control; temporary latrines etc. Trees and plants with flowers in the traditional mourning colours are planted, e.g. yellow allamanda, white spider lilies, purple thunbergia, white and yellow frangipani.

It must be emphasised that this brief description of current Chinese burial customs in Hong Kong represents no more than the observed practice at a particular point of time. Custom is a living body that changes gradually from generation to generation. It would therefore be unwise to assume that all these customs will survive. The impact of congestion, lack of burial space and improving social conditions in Hong Kong may well cause further changes. In particular, the proposed official encouragement of cremation as a means of disposal of the dead may do much to upset the current burial pattern, although it will follow the Buddhist practice more closely. The basic factor seems to be that Hong Kong Chinese are not so much concerned with the means of disposal of the dead as with being able to pinpoint the eventual resting place of the remains of the deceased, whether in the form of bones or ashes. Exhumation, as such, seems to play no significant part in the process except as a practical means of reducing the physical bulk of the deceased to proportions that will either fit into a funerary urn or below a horseshoe grave. Cremation, therefore, which serves the same practical purpose as exhumation in reducing bulk, should equally prove unobjectionable to Hong Kong Chinese, backed as it is by Buddhist belief. In short, one may expect that within a generation cremation may largely replace burial and exhumation as a means of customary disposal of Chinese dead in Hong Kong.